DA D0407614

– 64 –

Lessons for

a Life Without

Limits

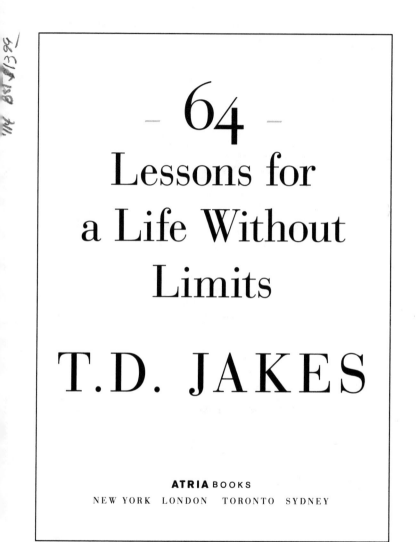

– 64 –
Lessons for
a Life Without
Limits

T.D. JAKES

ATRIA BOOKS

NEW YORK   LONDON   TORONTO   SYDNEY

ATRIA BOOKS

A Division of Simon & Schuster, Inc.
1230 Avenue of the Americas
New York, NY 10020

First Atria Books hardcover edition May 2011

ATRIA BOOKS and colophon are trademarks of Simon & Schuster, Inc.

For information about special discounts for bulk purchases,
please contact Simon & Schuster Special Sales at 1-866-506-1949 or
business@simonandschuster.com.

The Simon & Schuster Speakers Bureau can bring authors to your live
event. For more information or to book an event, contact the Simon &
Schuster Speakers Bureau at 1-866-248-3049 or visit our website at
www.simonspeakers.com.

Designed by Suet Y. Chong

Manufactured in the United States of America

10   9   8   7   6   5   4   3   2   1

Library of Congress Cataloging-in-Publication Data

Jakes, T. D.
    64 lessons for life without limits / T.D. Jakes. — 1st Atria Books
hardcover ed.
        p. cm.
1. Success—Religious aspects—Christianity. I. Title.
BV4598.3.J358 2011
248.8'4—dc22

                                                2011006237

ISBN 978-1-4516-2524-0
ISBN 978-1-4516-2525-7 (ebook)

Contents

SECTION 3

RESURRECT YOUR VISION

SECTION 4

PEOPLE POSSIBILITIES

SECTION 5

MONEY MONEY MONEY

SECTION 6

MINDFULLY RELATE AND MATE

SECTION 7

GET BACK UP AGAIN

SECTION 8

LIVE YOUR DREAM

Introduction

You've succeeded. You got it. You heeded that vague feeling that something in you needed to change. Or you may even have hit bottom in some aspect of your life and decided it was the last time! So you bought the books *Reposition Yourself* or *Making Great Decisions*, did the work, and slowly (or perhaps even with amazing speed), you and your situation have been transformed. Congratulations! You get the prize *and* the bag of chips.

Since I began writing books more than twenty years ago, I've been blessed to see my readers grow, their lives turn around. I'm humbled when they share that my books have ignited positive change, and I'm so proud of them when I hear their stories of success. As I've listened, I've learned that they are often surprised at how challenging it is to *maintain* the practices that led to their turnarounds. Years and years later, they often feel afraid to relax, concerned that they must constantly be vigilant, as if they are tiptoeing on eggshells and their accomplishments could somehow vanish.

If that's how you feel, this book is for you. It's about standing firm in who you have become, on what you have achieved. It is designed not to teach you new lessons but to build your confidence in what you have already learned.

I want you to embrace the *you* you have worked so hard to become, to *enjoy* the life your work has yielded. This book celebrates and affirms what you have absorbed and put into practice and helps you continue onward.

Should you ever feel yourself slipping or be painfully reminded of the person you used to be, remember that you *did* reposition yourself, that you *did* make good decisions and *did* follow a plan, and you *indeed* have a life without limits. Now stand firm.

—

Get a Reading of Your Reality

Know Who You Are and What You're All About

You are you wherever you are. Wherever you go, you take you with you. If you are kind and thoughtful to your friends and family, you are typically a kind and thoughtful employee as well. If you are the life of the office party and enthusiastically organize the secret Santa activities every year, then chances are you make things fun at home too. More often than not, our personalities are consistent across most of the areas of our lives.

So then, who are you? It seems like a simple question but is often one of the most challenging for people to answer. To know who you are and what you stand for, to be aware of how you are perceived by others and how you present yourself to the world is one of the most important aspects of a well-lived life. Your behavior in your public and private moments acts as your life's billboard, your personal brand.

Your brand consists of three attributes that are present for every encounter or meeting that you have with work colleagues, family, or friends. I like to call them "deliverables," virtues that you bring to all your social and business interactions. They aren't something that we get from a seminar or that we develop as we mature; deliverables are characteristics that are natural to you as a person and that reflect who you are as a person.

You may take your deliverables for granted. They seem second nature to you by now. But consider writing down or revisiting your own personal mission statement. What is your purpose on this planet? What are you about? What is your vision? Does your life truly reflect what is important to you and how you want others to see you?

So often, we live lives based on what those around us think we should be or do. We follow the path we've seen our friends, business associates, parents, or other family members take. Or we pursue what the media defines as success. Eventually, and sometimes surprisingly, we may find ourselves frustrated, angry, and disappointed in life. Have you ever heard business professionals lament about climbing to the top of the corporate ladder only to find that it was leaning against the wrong building? They were often so busy keeping up with what they thought they were supposed to be doing that they never stopped to ask themselves what they actually wanted to do.

By taking time to figure out your own personal brand, you make sure you are on the right path for you. You discover your unique deliverables. You develop a confidence in who you authentically are. What you learn about who you really are helps guide you throughout your life, no matter what circumstances or situations you find yourself in. Learn who you are, don't be deterred by the paths of others, honor your personal brand, and you'll never go wrong.

Assess Your Strengths and Weaknesses

One of the traits of successful, joyful living is understanding what you do well and knowing those areas where you may need assistance or support. Our strengths and weaknesses don't make us wrong or right, they make us who we are.

If you've ever heard the saying "No man is an island," it was probably said about a great leader. Few people achieve great success all on their own. Consider an actor in a play. He may be the one out front in the spotlight, with perfect hair, makeup, and costume, reciting poignant lines, and getting all the applause and accolades. But to get great reviews the day after opening night, he had to rely on the costume designer for the outfit he wore, the hair and makeup artists who made him look flawless, the playwright who wrote the words he said in his show-stopping soliloquy, the director who provided the vision, and the lighting and sound crews who set the stage. Great leaders are smart enough to surround themselves with people who have strengths that complement theirs. The leader is still in charge but has a team of supporters who help achieve the vision and goals.

You're a leader in some area of your life—home, family, your circle of friends, work, church—and you know that leadership has its challenges. While there are certainly many benefits to being in charge, at the same time leaders must often deal with conflict, controversy, and naysayers, who think they know better. One thing all leaders know is that while many people will never step up or out to be the leader, there are always plenty of folks willing to criticize any steps toward leadership you might take, and tell the whole world how they know better and why you did it wrong!

At work, you may take on the role of supervisor or assume leadership for a special project team. As the person in charge, you have the responsibility to thoughtfully assign tasks to team members, based on their strengths and interests, to build a group that will help you achieve the goals at hand. You may be surprised to later overhear a few complaints when you walk past the coffee break room. Your colleagues think they should have been awarded the job rather than you and may even set out to sabotage your efforts. The same may happen in family situations. Unfortunately, for a leader this comes with the territory. You can't let others keep you from achieving your goals. Not everyone will be your cheerleader all the time. That's just a fact of life.

You always want to treat people as you want to be treated, but you can't always count on being supported or even liked by everyone. And some people will be determined to be difficult and negative no matter what you do. You can never please everyone, but stay focused on your goals and always be who you are and you won't go wrong.

While they may mean well, sometimes family members can be negative as well. You may try to strike out on a new path, get an advanced degree or move to a new city, and they may try to stop you, saying things like "Why do you need to do that? No one in our family has ever lived there!" They may be afraid for you, or have a vision of you different from the one you have for yourself. Not everyone is going to understand or be supportive of the decisions you make. If you are a parent, for example, the best interest of your family is your number one priority. Your family looks to you for guidance and stability, not to be their buddy. Certainly having all the pay cable stations is more fun than paying the utility and grocery bills! While all the decisions you make may not be popular, leading the way based on who you are, spending household income responsibly, doing what you know to be best for the people who rely on you is your main concern. Real leaders make the tough decisions, even when it sometimes means they end up less than popular.

Leaders are secure in their vision for themselves. They know where they are going and don't let others deter them from their path. This doesn't mean that you won't face others who will try to get you off course and people who will try to convince you to take the easy or more popular route. The road to true leadership can sometimes feel lonely. But once you reach your goals, the rewards are enormous.

Follow your path, and don't allow coworkers, children, your spouse, friends, or anyone else to deter you from where you know you want to go. If you're going to be an effective leader, hold fast to your vision for yourself and employ the assistance of a great team of supporters to help you get where you want to go.

3

Accept Responsibility, Not Blame

Change is hard. That's just a fact of life. Bookstores are filled with popular self-help books that claim you can change your life in five or ten easy steps. But the truth is, it takes much more than that to make significant and lasting changes in your life. Change comes from consistent and focused hard work and effort. Sure, one in a million people gets lucky and wins Mega Millions, or is discovered waiting tables and becomes an instant star. The rest of us have to work at achieving our goals minute by minute, day by day, week after week, and year after year. The other important thing these "easy step" books don't tell you is that the road to success is not always a straight path. You will meet up with challenges and obstacles along the way.

Let's say your doctor has told you that unless you lose weight, you risk getting diabetes, like your mother and grandmother before you. You start off with the best intentions. You get yourself a gym membership and work out several times a week. You cut out sweets and other unhealthy foods, and you skip those late-night snack binges for weeks. You are looking better, feeling more energetic, and starting to feel good in your skin again, having lost ten pounds in just over a month.

Then one day your boss chews you out for being late with a report. You know the best thing to do is to head to the gym and get out your frustrations in your kickboxing class. But instead on your way home from work you drive right past the gym and head straight to the supermarket. You buy yourself some Ben & Jerry's Chocolate Fudge Brownie ice cream, and once home find yourself a spot on the sofa, turn on the TV, and eat the whole pint for dinner without one thought about the healthy salad you have waiting for you in the fridge.

When you are trying to make changes in your life, the fact is some days you are going to forget all about your goals of new, healthier habits. You are going to toss everything you learned, all the strides you've made, right out the window, and go right back to your old, bad habits. The key is to understand that a bad day is not a failure, it's not forever; it's just a bad day. Once you've had one, and everyone does, you simply start back on track the next day. Don't give up. Life is a series of stops and starts, ups and downs. Tomorrow is a new day.

Take responsibility for getting off track. While your boss may have yelled at you and that may have made you feel bad, he didn't force you to drive your car past the gym or hold the spoon of ice cream to your lips. You made the choice to give in to the upset and deal with it in the same old way. What is required now is to renew your vow to make changes in your life and begin from where you left off. Remind yourself of your vision for change, forgive yourself for whatever slipups you made, and begin walking forward again. Make your goal your focus, not the fact that you fell off the wagon. Don't get caught up with blaming your boss, or yourself. Acknowledge the behavior, let it go, and move on. Realize that the next time you come up against a stressful situation—and you will—you can handle it in a healthy manner. See yourself heading to the gym tomorrow after work and take that salad you have in the refrigerator with you and have it for lunch!

4

Take the Junk Out of Your Trunk—
And Save the Good Stuff

Have you ever seen the movie *Groundhog Day*? Bill Murray's character relives the same day over and over. As a movie it is funny, but in real life the idea is more sad than humorous. When we aren't aware of the patterns in our lives, we run the risk of repeating the same day in our lives over and over as well. Sometimes this is true in a work situation. We continually end up in jobs where we are overworked and underappreciated, or where we have an uncaring or belligerent boss who criticizes and belittles us in front of others. Or maybe our personal relationships always seem to be full of the same kind of drama. We repeatedly get involved with the person who is unfaithful or self-involved or unable to commit. The jobs may change, as may the partner, but the situation always seems the same. The divorce rate for second and third marriages is higher than for the first; perhaps unrecognized patterns are the reason.

If you are like many people, the trunk of your car can often serve as a metaphor for some of the stuff you are carting around in your life. You keep a small grill in there even though you rarely picnic. You may keep your golf clubs or other sporting equipment in there even though you almost never play these days. In order to move forward in life, you have to let go of old things and habits that no longer serve you. You have to clean the junk out of your trunk. That is the only way to clear space for the new things you desire in your life.

If you've seen my friend Niecy Nash and her program *Clean House,* you know exactly what I am talking about. Niecy and her team of cleanup and design experts descend on messy homes and work with the owners to get rid of the junk that is keeping them from truly living in their own homes. Most of the people are reluctant to let go of the old possessions that are clogging the rooms, closets, and floors of their homes even though the mess keeps them from enjoying being in their houses. Most of the time they don't even realize how attached they are to the junk, until Niecy and her team attempt to get them to throw it away. They want their house cleaned up, yet they cling to things from the past that keep them stuck in the mess they are in. Once they start to sell and throw out and let go, they clear up space to allow Niecy's team to clean and paint and decorate in a more modern, clutter-free, beautiful way, creating the opportunity for a new kind of life. What are you holding on to from your past that keeps you repeating the same patterns that keep you stuck?

The beautiful thing about ridding ourselves of the junk is that it enables us to see clearly what we want to keep. The "stuff" we save is what we truly cherish, and by making the keep-it decision, we affirm and acknowledge what is truly important. Who are the people in your life who really matter? What are the habits and practices that truly sustain you? Once we clear away who and what don't matter to us, we have the time and emotional space to savor what is not at all junk—whatever we have that is of enduring value.

5

Do an Internal Investigation

Relationships are important. Whether they be friendships, family relationships, or romantic ones, the people in our lives matter more than almost anything else. However, there is no more important relationship than the one we have with ourselves.

Knowing who we are and recognizing our limitations must happen before we ever try to partner with someone else. People often think that entering a relationship is about what you get, when the truth is relationships are equally about giving to others. Knowing what you would like in a partner begins with knowing who you are and why you want to be in a relationship. Jesus asks us, "Why do you look at the speck of sawdust in your brother's eye and pay no attention to the plank in your own eye?" (Matthew 7:3, NIV). In other words, we must consider how we see ourselves before we can look closely at the other person in our life.

Knowing who you are as a person and truly believing that you deserve love and attention from another person is the foundation block of self-worth. The ability to communicate that effectively and in a respectful manner is necessary to any healthy, mutually satisfying relationship. A sense of self-worth is not egotistical. It helps you set boundaries and ensures that no matter who you encounter, those standards will never be compromised. So often, when we experience frustration and feel taken advantage of in relationships, it is because we have allowed those boundaries to be crossed, or worse we never considered where the boundaries should be. The way to avoid this situation is to be clear who we are and what we are willing to do in a relationship. Ignoring the truth about another person or ourselves may be okay in the short run, but in the long term it generally leads to disaster. Ignorance in relationships is not bliss! With a strong foundation of knowing who you are and what you stand for, you will have the courage to ask the right questions and discern the answers. You will take in information and evidence that help you see who a person truly is and whether or not he or she fits into your life. You will be honest with yourself and others about who you are, what you want, and how you want to live your life.

Do you struggle with this issue of honesty in relationships? With the many changes in the roles of men and women in our society, many of both genders often wrestle with how to openly and honestly communicate with each other. Many have difficulty expressing feelings about themselves and their lives. Rather than being honest and open about who they are and what they want, they engage in short-term relationships, running for the door the moment a potential partner doesn't meet previously unexpressed expectations. The would-be mates in their lives routinely receive failing grades for tests they never know they are taking.

If you find that you have difficulty sustaining the long-term relationship you desire, consider if perhaps you have lacked the courage to express your true feelings and needs in relationships. Open, honest, meaningful conversation can feel intimidating if you are not used to it, but it is, in fact, what is required of sustained, meaningful relationships with all the people in our lives. You cannot realistically set expectations for other people without becoming intimately aware of who you are.

You may have heard the expression "We often dislike in others what we cannot accept in ourselves." The next time you feel ready to judge a potential partner for not being something you think you need, first ask yourself if you can find whatever you are looking for within and whether you have expressed that need in a way your potential partner understands and respects.

6

Everywhere You Go, There You Are

Your character is your foundation. It determines how you live your life, how you treat others, and how others respond to you. Without it, you are prone to flit about from here to there, distracted by whatever and whoever comes along, trying to be something different every day, creating drama wherever you turn.

People without good character are dangerous. They often use whatever power they have—be it small or great—in a negative way, spreading hurt and hate wherever they turn. Terrorists, tyrants, hatemongers of all kinds have one thing in common: they lack a strong and positive character.

Leaders motivate and enrich the lives of the people around them. Leadership is born from positive character traits and a healthy sense of self-esteem. Honesty, integrity, compassion, and a sense of self are all positive character traits that contribute to enduring leadership. People who lie, cheat, steal, oppress, or scream for accolades and recognition may enjoy momentary strides, but in the long term, they typically crash and burn.

The Bible says, "Renounce your sins by doing what is right, and your wickedness by being kind to the oppressed. It may be that then your prosperity will continue" (Daniel 4:27, NIV).

Success is garnered one step at a time, with the support of a good team, and without your hurting anyone else to get you where you are going. People who display true character at home and at the office, who work hard and share their successes with those who support them, and who put their faith in their Creator to walk along with them will be certain to accomplish everything they were meant to do.

Keeping up with the Joneses is never a productive use of time. "If your friend jumped off the bridge, would you follow?" is a question most of us were asked as children when we wanted to do what our buddies were doing. Yet as adults, we often get caught up in following the crowd, trying to keep up with the Joneses without ever asking ourselves if the Joneses are headed in a direction we want to go. The company we keep reflects who we are as people. If you find yourself hanging out with friends with questionable habits and behaviors, you may need to do a self-assessment on who you are.

You can have all the beautiful clothes, expensive shoes, and fancy cars in the world, but if you purchased them with credit cards and you can't afford to pay the bills when they arrive, then your appearance and likely your life are built on a foundation of lies, as may be your character.

If your character is not what you would like it to be, you have to be honest with yourself about where you are stuck and do what is necessary to break free from the old patterns that keep you making less than stellar choices. You cannot change what you won't acknowledge.

Like Moses, a criminal exiled from Egypt, discovered, seeing the truth about your situation and where you are in life is the first step toward making change. Once he heard the word of God and found his purpose, Moses built on that new foundation and became a leader. One of the reasons our church started the Texas Offenders Reentry Initiative (TORI) was to help young men and women rehabilitate their lives and find a new path. By placing people in an environment healthier than the one they are familiar with, we see their lives change dramatically. It's as if they are given a palette of fresh new paint with which they can create beautiful new pictures for their lives.

Overcoming difficult circumstances is not easy, but focusing on building up our character can help us transcend the most difficult of situations and free us up to make major changes in our lives that we can't yet imagine.

It is never too late to begin working on your character. Our environment has so much to do with who we become. If you are not happy with who you are in your current circumstances, then vow today to do something, no matter how small, to begin to change them. If you want to develop your character, hang out with people who are moving ahead and developing into the kind of people you admire. Associate with people who have the kind of commitment to excellence that you would like to have. Find someone who does what you want to do, who lives as you would like. If you can talk to them, ask them questions about how they got where they are, about how they do what they do. Then adapt what you learn to your life, find ways to put what you learn into action, work to develop the same kind of positive habits. Habits build character, and character is the foundation for a life of great success.

7

Balance the Twins Inside You

For many of us, our public face is very different from the face we show privately. It is almost as if there is a set of twins living inside us—fraternal, rather than identical twins. The self may look whole on the outside, but inside there is a war going on between these inner twins. One twin represents our ideal self, the positive, optimistic twin, whose character exemplifies all that we want to be and all we want the world to believe about us. The other twin is the real self, the more realistic representation of who we are. This twin is flawed, lacks effective communication skills, and is sometimes lazy or selfish. The twins are sometimes in conflict, the flawed twin often fighting to hide its shortcomings from the view of the world. As a result, we find that we are constantly at war with ourselves as well as with those around us. We're always trying to suppress that flawed self, keeping it from ourselves and the world.

The drive to live up to the expectation of the ideal self is exhausting. Dealing with external enemies can be hard enough; fighting them internally is even more frustrating. The internal fight is a daily struggle against who we really are. It is similar to what happens in our daily lives.

What we focus on in life is what expands. If we focus on our work life, we will probably get promotions and new assignments. If we focus on our home life, chances are it will grow stronger. But our home life may suffer from all the working hours we've had to put in, or if we are only focused on what happens at home, we may find ourselves at odds with our boss and work colleagues.

Most of us tend to need and want balance. Success in one area without success in the other is quite unsatisfying. You can be the greatest success in your work, but if you don't have friends and family to share the wealth of your accomplishment, then success often feels hollow. Achieving balance in life is challenging; there are only twenty-four hours in a day. Like the internal fight between our public and private selves, life is an ongoing project. Sometimes one aspect of life demands more from us. But if we can keep focused on our core values and who we know ourselves to be, then we will know at any particular time what should take precedence.

8

Know That Who You Are
Is Enough

To be young, attractive, smart, sexy, and hip, to be in the know and part of the cool club, all you need to do is to buy the latest smart phone and the hottest shoes, visit the newest club, or be seen at the right restaurant. At least that is what advertisers want us to believe. But as anyone who has bought a $600 pair of shoes that they couldn't afford knows, while they may look great with your outfit, they pinch the first day you wear them just like a pair from Payless.

Expecting a thing or an association with a certain group of people to make you feel good about yourself and who you are is fruitless. While you may look the part of smart, together, young sophisticate in your four-inch Prada pumps, you will still know that you don't feel good enough.

The only way to develop true self-love and confidence

is to embrace who you really are inside, to stand in your truth as an individual. This kind of self-understanding requires a lifetime of personal exploration and cannot be bought in a store, no matter how rich you are.

It is human nature to want to belong. C. S. Lewis, the British writer, delivered an address titled "The Inner Ring" describing this desire. He said it's an urge with which we all must wrestle, but he cautioned us to face what's at the core of this desire: our fear of being an outsider who must bear the pain of being rejected and alone. "As long as you are governed by that desire you will never get what you want. . . . Until you conquer the fear of being an outsider, an outsider you will remain."

Seeing your association with any group as a complement to your life's goals rather than an opportunity to define who you are is the healthiest approach to belonging. It is important to know who you are apart from others. Only then can you be completely open to receive whatever the organization has to offer you, without needing it to provide you with self-worth.

Who you are, a child of God, is all you need to be. Your associations with others offer you community, friendship, a chance to connect with others, but your worth as a person comes from inside.

—

Recalibrate
Your Life

9

Identify What Matters Most

Incorporate your family and loved ones into each and every stage of your life, whether it's ascending, leveling off, or descending.

Learn to take the excitement of your career and public pursuits into your home and share it with those who are committed to you and your well-being. They want to be a part of whatever it is you are going through if you will only let them. Focus on relationships first. Take time with the ones you love instead of time with ones you can barely tolerate! There's an often-repeated quote in Mario Puzo's *The Godfather,* that one should keep friends close and enemies closer, but that's not the way of the true God. Keep your friends close and your family even closer.

Like the pilot who has trouble connecting the moving vehicle with the stable ground, you need direction from the control tower. I believe that God is in the tower to help you regain alignment. Your spiritual life can assist you in finding a stable place to balance your turbo-charged life. Emphasizing the spiritual can help you fit into a world that you may feel disconnected from or only mildly involved in.

This is why I believe that faith is so critical. Only God, who sits in the control tower, can show you how to re-align what you did in the air with who you are at home. It is through spiritual direction that you will be positioned for a safe and satisfying landing—a landing into the welcoming arms of a life that is not dependent on what you have accomplished materially or publicly. I am talking about someone who waits for you and sees you as more than what fans or coworkers see. These are not colleagues who love you for what you do. These are people who value you for who you are. It is with them that you want to land. But you cannot land if you haven't any runway left to hold you as you come in for a landing. What will it profit you to gain this whole world and lose your soul? If you lose those you love, what good are all the rest of your accomplishments?

The love and shared moments are the only parts of you that you can truly take with you when you depart from this life and begin your final descent. You can't take your sports cars or your latest designer bling, your luxury condo in the islands or your portfolio. Only the things that matter most can accompany you on your next journey, and none of them are material things. I challenge you to do what you must do today to reposition your priorities and take your pursuit of success into your home. Remind the people in your life why you're doing what you do outside the house by sharing your heart, your time, and your concerns with them. Let them in and keep them on board the flight with you. It will make your time in the air so much more meaningful and enjoyable and will guarantee a smooth landing in a destination that already feels like where you belong.

10

Decide to Stay in It to Win It

Few successful people got where they are without over-coming some serious challenges. We may see the fruits of their labor in terms of a bestselling product, a long tenure at the top of a Fortune 500 company, or a celebration with their teammates on the winners' podium. But the road to great fortune is typically a long one. Winners know that the way to accomplish their goals is rarely a straight path, and they learn to adapt to stops, starts, changes, and setbacks early on.

In his popular book *Good to Great: Why Some Companies Make the Leap . . . and Others Don't,* business leader and author Jim Collins compares mega grocery stores A&P, the largest retailing organization in the world in the 1950s, and Kroger, a small, value-based chain of supermarkets also thriving in the fifties. He reviews how both companies saw the world as they knew it changing as technology began to evolve during the 1960s. Smartly, both companies conducted research and hired highly qualified analysts to forecast how these changes would impact future business, and they each concluded that going forward, convenience would be paramount. One-stop shopping was the name of the new shopping game, and Kroger took steps to adjust its stores to the new "superstore" strategy we take for granted today. In addition to food, they started to carry toiletries, prescription drugs, household items, and more. A&P, however, chose to ignore the findings. In 1999, Kroger generated profits eighty times that of its onetime competitor A&P and took over the number one spot.

Like the beloved Sam Cooke song says, "Change Is Gonna Come." Change is inevitable in business and in life, and how you react to it is the key to your level of success. Nimbleness and flexibility are traits you will need to achieve your dreams, along with a commitment to your goals and a willingness to fight with intention to make them happen. When something goes wrong or challenges come up, don't flail around hysterically searching for a solution. You can't underestimate the power of stopping and taking a long, deep breath. Take a moment to refocus on your goals. Think about where you are trying to go. Ask for help if you need to, get all the information, and then make a calm, informed decision about what to do next. Then set back out on your path with new information and experience under your belt.

To achieve all you want in life, you can't afford to ignore the signs of change or oncoming challenges. Pretending something isn't happening is simply living in denial. Do you have the tools to adapt to change when it comes? Are the techniques you use to cope proactive and effective? Planning ahead for those inevitable changes, learning to stop, breathe, and refocus, and developing a support team of people in your field will help you be ready.

Get Your Life Off Flatline

Once we meet the typical milestones of life—graduate from school, get married, maybe have a few children, or reach a certain level of success in our chosen fields—we often start to think that's it for life, our best years are behind us. On the surface our life appears fulfilling. It may not be terribly exciting but we know what to expect; it's comfortable in a predictable kind of way. But when many people reach this place, something still feels not quite right. They wonder, What happened to some of those unfulfilled dreams? We read a great book and recall that we once wanted to write a novel. Or we hear a beautiful aria and remember how we once loved to sing. Dreams get buried but they never really die. That little flutter you feel when you hear that beautiful song as you drive down the freeway on your way home from work is that dream gasping for air.

Sometimes our zest for life gets suffocated by the demands and stresses of everyday life. Business trips, weekend soccer practice, family obligations, tuition bills, and mortgage payments sometimes make dreams seem frivolous and out of reach. We get downright weary from what can become the heaviness of life. Disconnection from our spouse, the exhausting demands of children, and the drama of teenagers can sometimes make life feel like a giant treadmill, and we just trudge along without feeling like we are making much progress. Unfortunately this is often the time in life when many people begin to self-destruct in order to combat feelings of disappointment and boredom or to escape their frustration. They make poor choices like having an affair, making an uninformed financial investment, or buying an expensive new sports car. Many people live lives of quiet desperation stuck in the mud of mediocrity.

Mediocrity is like a terrorist threat against our daily lives. It steals moments from our day, sabotages opportunities for advancement and personal growth, and takes away our desire for meaning. It transforms our lives into weapons of mess and destruction. The word *mediocre* means accepting the second-rate, the average (or below average), that which is middling, ordinary, commonplace, and run-of-the-mill. Rather than strive to resurrect those buried dreams, mediocrity wants you to resign yourself to the middle of the road.

Have you heard the whisper of the demon of mediocrity? It says things like "You can't go back to school now, you are too old!" Or "You don't have the money to open your own business!" Or "Who would want you, with your cellulite and false teeth?" Mediocrity sends people over to tell you how stupid you are to consider giving up your secure job for one in a new field, or how ungrateful you are for not being satisfied with all you have, or how you will fail if you try something new. It makes you think that where you are may not be great, but it is good enough, why make waves? And you hear it so often that you begin to believe that you truly are at the end of the road, that there really is nothing more than this.

But then there's still that little inkling. . . . Every time you drive past the university or see your daughter's college textbooks sitting on the kitchen counter or hear that beautiful aria, you wonder, *What if?*

Do you really think the Creator meant for you to feel resigned about the gift of life? Sure, you have obligations and responsibilities that you must take care of each day, but putting aside a little personal time to dust off one of those dreams or goals could be the most productive thing you can do to put a little spring back in your step and resurrect your enthusiasm for life. Taking just one step—like signing up for a class at the local community college one night a week, or joining the church choir—could be just the thing you need to remedy those feelings of malaise. Getting back in touch with those things that matter to you can go a long way toward reviving your enthusiasm for other areas of your life and starting you off on a long but joyous journey toward your dream.

12

When Your Life Gets Off Course, Recalibrate

Sometimes the distance between what you dream and what you see as achievable feels like a thousand miles. We may know that we are off course in our life but we are not sure what to do to get back on track. Who we know we are on the inside does not match how we are living, and we don't know what to do. Many of us have turned away from the life we know we are meant to live and must get back in touch with who we really are, our essence, our God-given gifts.

When that feeling nags at you, it's time to reposition yourself and figure out who you have become and where you are. It may mean you have to confront certain things you may not like about yourself and your current situation.

Starting the process is the hardest part. One way that I've seen work for many people is to stop seeing yourself as you or others see you, and see yourself as God does. Step outside yourself and focus on your gifts as the Creator sees them. Our vision for ourselves and life's possibilities is one of the first things that fades away when life gets hard, when we get bogged down in illness or debts or sadness. But get back in touch with that vision, and you will start to live your dreams with your eyes wide open!

And where you see a disconnection between who you really are and how you are living, let go of the blame and self-recrimination for getting off track. Once you do, you will begin to notice that what is inside is now on the outside, manifesting in your life. Who you are behind closed doors becomes who you are everywhere.

Allow yourself to see yourself as fresh and new, ready to begin again. Take what you know from the wrong turns of the past and use them as learnings, not lashings. Start walking forward one step at a time. When you view yourself as God does, you see yourself standing up to say, "I am here and ready to use my gifts to live the life I was destined for!"

13

Anticipate Change

Time brings change. With every passing second we age, the tilt of the earth changes, and the clock ticks one moment later. Yet we often cling to people and things as if we can stop time from passing and keep everything the same. Trying to stop change only leads to frustration and despair, because it literally cannot be done. But what you can do is plan to be ready to deal with it when it happens. You may not be able to predict what the change will be, but you can put things in place that will help you deal with it when it arrives.

Children will one day go to college, so wise parents consider saving when their babies are first born. Young people will one day stop working, so it makes sense to save for retirement. The elderly will eventually pass on, and the prudent make funeral arrangements and have a will in place. A CEO, who will one day step down, plans for a successor so the company can continue to flourish.

Sometimes change is hard, but planning helps us greet change. Use your own personal GPS to look ahead in your own life, and program it to reach your destination. And don't be afraid to go off the course, if necessary, and chart a new path that no one else has driven down before. With God at your side, you have all the tools you need for success, including the flexibility and adaptability to adjust your course whenever necessary.

You can be a pioneer of change in your own world. Long before Dr. King's birthday was declared a national holiday by our government, Dr. Martin Luther King was hated and resented and barred from speaking before many of the organizations that now embrace and celebrate him. Today he is revered as an icon of American history. Dr. King was a champion of change. He was a visionary who saw the world far beyond the civil rights movement. And just as things were not easy for Dr. King, they won't always be easy for you. At every turn there will be obstacles and people who will want to get you off course. To withstand the naysayers—or even worse, the sometimes brutal attacks that agents of change, like Dr. King, endure—you will need courage and conviction to stay on your path.

Innovation is often the catalyst behind change, but it is also a balm for the challenges of change. Think of how technology such as cell phones and computers have literally changed the way we shop, the way we communicate, and the way we live. The GPS is an amazing technological innovation that some map designers were none too happy to embrace, but it has transformed the experience of finding one's way while driving. As you pioneer change in your world, reach out for the latest tools and techniques, whether they be technological or involve new approaches to your family life, diet, exercise, or spirituality.

Plan for the Unexpected

You've heard the expression, "The best-laid plans of mice and men often go awry." It is true. No matter how well you prepare and plan, stuff happens! Relationships change, circumstances end, life switches course in a heartbeat. One minute you are working in your dream job; the next you find yourself standing in the unemployment line.

Life is beautiful, but the swiftness of change, especially unwanted change, can knock us off our feet and leave us wondering what hit us. We all face trials and tribulations; it is impossible to live without them. Even being the most faith-filled, financially responsible, giving individual won't prevent you from experiencing unexpected change.

But some people seem to handle change better than others. While some of us get knocked down and out, others get back on their feet swiftly, throwing punches at whatever tried to take them out. It isn't that these people don't suffer the pain and sadness that often accompanies life's tragedies, but they appear to have a secret weapon that helps them not only recover but get back on the path with little drama and angst. While many of us are still whining about what went wrong and how life is unfair, those who have prepared for the unexpected are thriving, living large, seemingly without effort. And it's not that they take a Pollyanna, life-is-always-wonderful view of life: they are truly ready to take on the world again.

Thrivers have a mind-set that gives them an edge even in the face of difficulty. By refusing to accept defeat, successful people see everything that happens in life as a learning experience, a chance to expand as a person. You can transform adversity into opportunity with the right approach.

Losing a loved one suddenly is about as awful an experience as we can have. Particularly when someone we know is vibrantly alive, it is hard to accept suddenly that we will never hear their voice or feel their touch ever again. But I know plenty of people who use that terrible experience as a wake-up call to live their lives to the fullest. They treat the people who remain in their lives with more love and kindness, knowing full well that tomorrow is never guaranteed. They use their lives as a kind of monument to those who have left them, vowing to live their lives fully because their loved ones no longer have the opportunity.

Thrivers are conditioned to prevail no matter what the circumstances. They are trained to be conquerors. Even when they lose everything, they display a seemingly indefinable gift for making lemonade out of lemons. They see pains and failures of the past as lessons, not reasons to hide from life. They see their lives as limitless and relentlessly work to reach their goals no matter what happens, first because they have the right attitude, and second because they are prepared.

Thrivers save money to pay for emergencies; they take classes to learn what they can about new products and technology; they keep their relationships and contacts fresh and current so that when they need to call someone for help, the someone they call gladly picks up the phone! It's like the spare tire and the tools in your trunk for changing a flat. You hope you don't ever need them, but if you drive, you keep them clean and full of air and ready to go just in case you hit that bump in the road.

15

Maintain Your Launching Pad

What is your source of strength? For many of us it is our families. When we come up against difficult situations, it is often our families that we turn to for comfort and support. It is to the arms of our families that we go to recover, rejuvenate ourselves, and then our families are the base from which we strike back out into life.

When the entire family shares our vision and dreams, each member has an important role to play in helping us reach our goals. We need that base of support for encouragement and help. Suppose Dad goes back to school at night, with a dream of getting the master's degree he had to put aside to support his kids. Now, many years later, the whole family gets into the act. So he can go to classes after work, Mom takes a second job, the kids pitch in with chores and help make dinner, everyone works together to help Dad get that diploma, and the whole family shares in the graduation! Sure, the house was a little less clean while Dad was in school, and dinner was often frozen fish sticks and french fries, but when people love you, they are willing to sacrifice, because your dreams become theirs.

So often, though, when one member of a family group steps out to do something out of the ordinary, the result is friction and dissent. Members can grow resentful and feel taken advantage of, feeling their needs aren't being met. Love is sometimes not enough to smooth the way for change, and sometimes people grow apart. In order to benefit from supporting your dream, your family must continue to grow together in love and as people.

Achieving dreams doesn't happen overnight. Each family member must feel like a part of the team for any one individual to succeed. Regular communication is essential: family gatherings and meetings to check in with how each member is doing in the pursuit of individual and family goals. Sharing thoughts and feelings is vital to your personal success as well as the success of your family unit. The family is the launching pad from which every member can soar.

16

Find Your Personal Route
to Prosperity

I am often called the professor of the P-word, as in prosperity. I don't like it, but there's not much I can do about the label. The term is used to criticize certain religious leaders, but I don't believe there is such a thing as the so-called prosperity gospel, nor do I embrace the label of "prosperity preacher."

Like the path to success, the path to prosperity is not, I believe, a straight line that can be mapped on a graph by a motivational guru, business tycoon, or life coach who writes a bestselling self-help book. Everyone who has followed my ministry knows that I have written and sold a lot of books, invested wisely, bought and sold countless properties, and written and produced music, plays, and movies, and I have prospered. But my success is the result of a combination of God's grace and a lot of hard work. I have used my ministry to encourage and uplift people who were emotionally, socially, or sexually abused. As a Christian, I know there is only one Gospel and it is in the context of faith: God's grace extended through the death, burial, and resurrection of our Lord.

There is no such thing as a prosperity gospel. Prosperity has no bible, nor is it a gospel unto itself. God's promise to us is eternal life, not eternal cash or riches. Giving is just one part of the economic equation, and I believe that to teach that as the primary mechanism of financial empowerment only leads to disappointment. Only a very small percentage of my teaching ministry focuses on finances. When I do talk about finances, it is usually to say that if God can bless me with skills and resources, then he can help anyone build and shape their life.

I know the road out of poverty is not easy. In order to walk that road, you must believe that you are empowered by God to overcome your circumstances.

But faith is only part of what you need. A necessary part, but as the Bible says, without work, faith is only an idea. Faith only works when you work it. You must give your faith a life by doing the hard work to achieve what you believe. Do you have an understanding of the route you are to follow out of poverty, debt, lack? If not, pray, and then get off your knees and reposition yourself, knowing God will guide you.

———

Resurrect
Your Vision

17

Resurrect Your Dream

God wants us to have dreams. He wants us to see the world as we did as kids, full of possibilities and chances to be who we were meant to be. Unless we want to spend the rest of our lives feeling unfulfilled and uninspired, we have to take the dreams out of the closet and blow the dust off!

It's easy to get caught up in "have tos" and the responsibilities of life—working, caring for children, spouses, and aging parents, taking care of homes, and so on. But you must believe that you can resurrect your life and your dreams; you must have faith that you have the ability to tap into the enthusiasm you once felt for life.

To hope requires faith, faith in God and faith to begin again. You must have the courage to face the disappointments of the past and take a good look at how you got off the path to where you were headed. Then you have to silence the voice in your head that will show up when you least expect it, saying, *This is all there is* or *Who are you to want more from life?* or *You can't do it; it's too late for you.* We give up our dreams because we think that's what grown-ups are supposed to do. But as we mature, we realize that reaching for our dreams is what makes us feel alive and helps us stay connected with our lives.

If you have children, consider what a blessing watching you pursue a dream would be for them. Knowing what you know now, you can be the example they need to ensure that they don't settle for less than fulfillment in their own lives. Imagine how wonderful you will feel going after what you dream of. Envision the positive effect you could have on your marriage and other relationships, as you live your dream. Get back in touch with your life's purpose and those activities that once brought you great joy and satisfaction.

As with Lazarus, whom Jesus brought back to life, God can restore your dreams. With love, prayer, and great attention, your dreams, like Lazarus, can be resurrected from the grave in which they've been buried. If you can dream it, you can achieve it.

The secret to recapturing dreams is to enjoy the pursuit of the dream, rather than to focus on the outcome. Achievement in this case is not position, title, fame, or financial compensation. Achieving your dreams means doing what you love. No, you will never be the star running back in the NFL, especially with your bad knees! But you can coach the local kids' team. You may never dance in the Houston Ballet, but you can take lessons on weekends and perform in the adult student recital. You may need to do some rethinking and repositioning, but your dreams never really have to die.

18

Be a Make-It-Happen Person

You dream about something. You have faith in God. Now put a strategy in place to make those dreams happen. Take them out of your head and make concrete, small steps toward them.

We may see other people achieve the kinds of things we wish we could—buying homes, starting businesses, enjoying relationships—and get upset, thinking, *They aren't as smart or as capable as we are. How could they achieve where we haven't?* we wonder. What we don't know is that those people had a plan. We work hard like they had to work hard, but they worked smart: they worked according to a plan. We never see what they sacrificed for the things they've achieved. From the outside, people's accomplishments may look as if they were simple to achieve, but from the inside out, the situation is likely very different.

Do some homework, put together a plan, and ready

yourself for success. For example, buying a house was important to me. My parents taught me that home ownership was one of the roads to wealth. When I bought my first home, I had a strategy. My credit wasn't great and my resources were limited. I had to make a plan and implement it. I started developing relationships with people at my local bank. I worked to reduce my debt, sacrificing and saving every way I could. I did everything possible to put myself in line with the move I wanted to make next. Eventually, it happened; I bought my first home.

Have you ever been watching television or reading a newspaper or magazine and seen a program or an ad for a product and exclaimed to yourself, "That was my idea!" Ideas only become a reality when we take the steps to get them out of our head and into the real world. The person who developed the product or wrote the screenplay that you "thought of first" created the business plan or took the screenwriting class or took any of the countless other steps necessary to bring an idea to fruition. And that's what you have to do to get ready to see your dream come true.

Too many of us take a passive approach to our lives, turning over the job of living to God, the doctor, parents, spouses, or whomever else we see as in charge of our life. You and only you are responsible for living the life you envision for yourself. God is of course always walking with you, offering you support and guidance, but he can't work unless you are working too! Remember the man lying beside the healing waters of Bethesda (John 5:5–15)? He asks Jesus to help him to the water so that he can be healed. But Jesus questions his resolve. Jesus is not being dismissive or uncaring, but he wants the man to understand that he has everything he needs within him to walk again. The man was waiting for someone to come along and help him, when instead of waiting, he should have been planning how to get well.

Yes, we all worry about what will happen if we try and fail. You've heard the old saying "It's better to have loved and lost than never to have loved at all." The principle applies to other aspects of life as well. If you never take the chance and go after what you want, then you can be certain that you will never achieve it. Failure is actually a very good teacher. Make a plan. Work your plan. If it fails, figure out why and make a revised plan, and work it again.

Make-it-happen people are planner-doers. They start with dreams and ideas, then they make preparations to achieve the things they want in life. Failure is never a concern because they know that with God and hard work, they will do what it takes to make their dreams happen.

19

Be the Captain of
Your Own Destiny

Living in a society inundated with reality shows and celebrity gossip blogs, it is easy to think that there is a wealthy benefactor, a billionaire businessman, a bachelor or bachelorette, or a plastic surgeon who is going to sweep in and take care of all our needs. But what the people on these modern-day fairy tales don't seem to reveal is that life is what you make it. You are the one responsible for your destiny. When you place your life in the hands of someone else, you relinquish your personal power. It may seem easier to pass on the responsibilities of your life to someone else, but in the long run it's a mistake.

Sure, as the captain of your ship, you are the one to blame when things go wrong or fall apart, but you are also large and in charge when they go well. You can re-bound from any mistakes you've made in the past and overcome challenges and obstacles when you know that you have the power to do so. And you come into that power by taking responsibility for your life. You must take responsibility for your future and step out on a path that will help you prosper in every aspect of your life.

God knows life is not always fair. We live in a world where systematic injustice is still a reality for many people. We have our first African American president, but we still have a long way to go in this country before we can truly say that all God's children enjoy the same liberties. But when we are unhappy with our station in life, blaming others about the past or the world's inequities is not only exhausting, it's simply counterproductive. Focusing on what's wrong and what may not change anytime soon is not how to get ahead in life. Remain true to God and to who you are, and empower yourself by stepping out in faith toward the life you want each day.

Standing on your own personal responsibility, taking care of yourself and your family in the best way you can, being an honest, upright citizen of the world, treating others as you want to be treated—that is what puts you in charge of your own destiny. And it will contribute to the world's being a better place.

It is the responsibility of each of us, as citizens of the world, to stand up against injustice wherever we see it. Whether it's at the country club, at the local private or public school, at the senior citizens' home, at the grocery store, at the local pool, or in our own homes, we are obligated to stand up for justice and for our neighbors no matter what their skin color. Dr. King said, "The ultimate measure of a man is not where he stands in moments of comfort and convenience, but where he stands at times of challenge and controversy." At the end of each day, when you look at yourself in the mirror, ask yourself where you stand—first on the basic issues of personal responsibility, then on matters of social responsibility.

20

Cultivate an Attitude of Gratitude

Being thankful is one of the best ways I know to be successful in life. When you are conscious of the many blessings bestowed on you, then you not only look to enjoy them for yourself, but you want to share them with others. People often think that a spirit of contentment means that you no longer strive for a better life. Nothing could be further from the truth. True gratitude is an understanding that if you are not happy just as things are now, a big bonus check won't likely change anything for the better. As we read in 1 Timothy 6:6, "But godliness with contentment is great gain" (NIV).

Be who you are in God's eyes and don't identify yourself by the obstacles in your way. Focusing on the blessings we have in our lives, showing gratitude for the gifts we already possess, frees us from feeling "less than."

Be grateful for what you already have and take steps

to improve your financial situation with the knowledge that material things don't determine who you are. Go back to school to get the skills or the degree that will help you increase your salary and get the promotion at work, and balance that effort by acting on plans that will allow you to put aside money for your children's education or other purposes. You are not motivated by greed or desire for status. You are, rather, appreciating who you are and what you have right now. That keeps you from wanting and buying things you can't afford in the belief that doing so will make you feel better about yourself.

Many of us, particularly those who grew up in less than wealthy environments, have an addiction to poverty. It is a mentality that can keep us stuck in deprivation and lack. We overspend to keep up with the Joneses, or we blow our money on nonnecessities when we can't even pay our monthly bills. While we may secretly yearn to own a home or return to school, we believe that sort of success in life—a comfortable home or a good job—is for other people but not for us. We do things that constantly keep us in debt, financially and psychologically.

Advertising is a significant part of our culture. We are constantly bombarded with ads for products and services everywhere we turn. Most of us can't afford to buy these things we are told will make us better people. So how do we protect ourselves from feeling we need these products to be accepted and okay?

If you feel "less than" financially, the place to begin is not with attaining more things or even more money. Rather focus on what you already have, no matter how little it may seem. Start where you are by sitting down with a list of your monthly expenses and give thanks for the income you have, whether it covers your bills or not. With an attitude of gratitude, make out a realistic budget. Now with a true financial picture in place, you can make informed purchases and develop a plan for where you want to be tomorrow.

If you already have a plan in place, consider how you might adjust the plan to be more effective in getting you where you want to go. Take a look at what's working for you and what isn't. If you haven't developed a plan yet, there's no time like the present. Approach your life with a sense of urgency. Life is short. Sticking your head in the sand to avoid facing your situation is not the answer. Financial mistakes and debt are like a cancer; they will spread and take over your life, as the disease will attack the body. The cure is a healthy attitude of appreciation for what you *do* have, and then a clear strategy for achieving your goals in a systematic manner.

There is no time like the present to change your life. With God at your side and a plan in place, you have the tools to look back a year from now and be grateful for how far you've come.

21

Prepare Yourself for the Doors That Are Opening for You Now

When you move, there are steps you must take to be ready on moving day. You call and arrange a date for the movers to come; you switch the phone, electric, and cable to your new address; you wrap your belongings in bubble wrap and newspaper and place them in boxes marked kitchen items, bedroom items, and living room items.

The process to get yourself ready for the next phase of your life journey is similar. You're moving up! You must prepare in advance in order to be ready to go forward with ease into the next phase of your successful life. Here are some shorthand preparation tips to follow so you will stand ready for whatever doors in life open for you.

- Create a plan for financial independence. This includes retirement, estate, and insurance planning. Research and implement a sound investment plan to help you ensure your financial future. (Insurance is the kind of thing we buy and hope we will never have to use, but it is a necessary expense. Your insurance policy should also cover your mortgage in case you become sick or incapacitated, or for some other reason are not able to work. You can be speeding along down the road of life when suddenly you suddenly hit an oil patch and skid off the road. You don't want to wait until a crisis strikes before you think of preparing yourself and your family for it.)

- Today's workers change careers many times. You may decide, after you've run the first half of the marathon that is life, to change directions and swim or bike the rest of the way. Always allow yourself flexibility. What you want to do now may be very different from what you will want to do twenty years from now or what you wanted to do twenty years ago. What is so wonderful about life is that no matter how old you are, you can always start again, and opportunities may exist later that you can't foresee now.

- Hobbies are important to nourish our souls. Consider hobbies that will allow you to meet people with whom you want to associate. A good deal of business is done on the golf course and on the tennis court, so a hobby can also contribute to your professional life.

- Technology is a major part of modern society. There's no getting around it. Those who aren't up to date and able to utilize the latest technological tools will have a hard time being successful. In addition to technology, it is important that you stay abreast of the latest developments in other kinds of business skills as well. Negotiation, communication, and etiquette are all necessary to succeeding in a changing world.

You are ready to step through the door to your new life. Think outside the box, do differently than you have done before, but remain who you are in your traditional values, and your life will soar to heights like you can't imagine.

22

Do Whatever It Takes and Stay on Top of Your Game

One of the things you will find in common among successful business people and anyone else who has achieved a dream is that they were willing to do what's necessary to meet their goals. They were willing to humble themselves, be creative, and go further than they ever have before. They took the steps other people weren't willing to take, worked the extra hours, skipped the parties and invitations, and sacrificed in order to succeed.

Once some reach a certain level of success, they find that happiness still eludes them. Now able to afford more expensive items than they once could, nicer clothes and cars, they stop growing. Very prosperous people can find themselves just as unhappy, if not more so, as they were when they were broke. The truth is many people come to realize that it was the climb that made them feel fully alive. When they reached the top of the mountain, there was nowhere else to go. So it's key that you continue to give yourself somewhere to go, something else to accomplish.

A midlife crisis is what we commonly call this phenomenon of high achievers feeling empty and lost. Is success really meaningful if you've done everything necessary to get to the top, yet you know in your soul that there are other things you were meant to do?

That's the time for transformation! Rather than cling to past success, as if we will never go any higher, we have to ask ourselves if our hearts are still in what has led to our success. If the answer is no, then it's time to refocus.

This is not to say that you need to make an abrupt change to be happy and satisfied in life. Staying on top of your game may happen as a natural flow into a new experience, a higher level of freedom and fulfillment. If you block the inner feeling that you are no longer doing your best, you will not be at peace with your success, no matter how hard you worked to get there. It is precisely because of your willingness to work and sacrifice that you will feel like something is missing.

23

Be Prepared for the Challenges of Success

Success is a wonderful by-product of hard work and focus. It enables you to enjoy many benefits that make life more comfortable, and it presents new challenges, many in particular that result from your increased wealth, stature, and visibility.

You can't do it all alone. The more successful you become, the more you need others you trust to help you manage your growing responsibilities and widening sphere of influence.

There are two groups of people drawn to the successful—handlers and carriers. The handlers deal with you out of necessity. They try to associate themselves with you for their own gain. But they may not have your best interest at heart or hold themselves to a high standard in the work they do for you. How many times, for example, have we heard of famous people filing for bankruptcy after handing over their fortunes to some-one who was mishandling their money? You, not your ac-countant, should be in charge of your finances.

Carriers, on the other hand, have your best interest as their number one concern. They take pride in their work on your behalf. They pick you up when you're down and carry on when you're too tired. They become partners in your success. Carriers will empower you and support you in remaining true to who you are and what you want from life. They will keep you growing and expanding and standing in your truth as a child of God.

We are all handled at one time or another, but if you have more handlers than carriers in your life, you may find yourself busy all the time but notice that for all the activity, you aren't moving forward.

Surround yourself with people who can help carry you and who will help you manage the inevitable han-dlers in life.

— 24 —

You're Part of a Unique
Intergenerational Masterpiece

The opportunities for your life are endless, secured by
the rich heritage of your ancestors. Whatever your ethnic-
ity, your ancestors sacrificed so that you could be all you
were meant to be in life.

Don't hide your history. Know it, understand it, and
celebrate it. Build on the wisdom of your grandparents,
your aunts and uncles and cousins, and continue creating that intergenerational masterpiece that is your life
and your history. Pass the legacy on to your children, so
they too understand the strength of the shoulders on
which they stand. We each have a responsibility to take
our family story to the next level. It is not enough to rest
on the accomplishments of the generations that came before us.

Our lives are a precious gift and every ancestor is a
teacher, whatever that ancestor's particular issues and

challenges were. Think about what each one had to offer. Mother may have cooked for the family and then taken a plate of food to the elderly widow next door. Aunt Sadie and Uncle Joe may not have had children of their own, but she taught Sunday school, while he started a Boy Scout troop. Your cousins saved their pennies and, rather than spending on candy for themselves, donated the money to help buy Christmas gifts for children at the orphanage. Individually these may seem like small actions, but when you look at them all together, they become the family story—your story and the foundation of your community.

Community cannot exist without unity. People coming together for the common good, despite what separates them, is what unity is all about. The key to true prosperity is to pass on to the next generation what you have inherited. "Pay it forward" is not just a catchy idea, it is the basis for living a truly balanced life rich with many blessings.

No matter what your heritage, it is a masterpiece, albeit imperfect. It contains oil paints and pastels and watercolors too. It has various brushstrokes. The perspective is likely off in some places, and there are shadows in places where they don't belong. Those who came before you likely had to face trials as difficult, or more so, than what you face. Their pains may be your pains, but their victories are yours also. Your challenge is to add your marks to the masterpiece—to have something to hand down to the next generation.

—

People
Possibilities

25

Begin Before "Need" Has You

Companionship is among our basic human needs. Most of us would find life sad and lonely without that all-important interaction with other people. While there are those among us who prefer a solitary life, most of us are social beings who are at our best around others. We garner energy and support from our connections. For some, a special someone in their life is all they need. Others thrive in groups that support them and give them a feeling of belonging.

On the other side of the coin are those who feel a sense of shame or embarrassment for admitting their loneliness. We may long for people to share our lives with but feel we have to pretend that we don't need anyone. It has become unfashionable in our modern society to say out loud that we'd like a companion or that we want other people in our lives. While your single friends may pat you on the back for keeping things "light and loose," the truth is most of us do better in life in concert with others. You should not feel any shame for wanting love and social connection. Rather than signifying weakness, admitting your desire to be loved and taking the step toward involvement actually require a great deal of courage. Accepting that you are a person who needs to connect is healthy.

Problems arise, though, when the need for companionship controls you and defines who you are. When you enter into relationships compromising yourself and your values in order to be with someone, the results are negative. Clinging to other people without an understanding of who they are or what they represent is unhealthy, and the ramifications can have not only life-long effects; they can sometimes have life-threatening consequences.

Smart decisions about relationships are never to be made in a mind-set ruled by fear of loneliness or by desperation. If that's where you are, then being single is a better alternative for you right now. It need only be temporary. The key is to admit that you want a relationship and proceed to lead a life consistent with the values you'd want your loved one to hold dear as well.

Relationships with people should be an important part of your life, and those relationships start with what you have to give and share with others, rather than with your unmet needs.

26

Decide with Whom You Will Share Your Influence

We are often known by association. As you rise through the ranks of your company or achieve recognition in your community or other endeavors, you must be conscious of carefully choosing the people with whom you associate.

People will often use connections to expand their own sphere of influence. Like the glossy flyers advertisers place in the center of the Sunday paper, people sometimes work to insert themselves into your life and try to gain attention and influence by a perceived association with you. They don't really want an honest relationship with you; they just want what they think they can get by associating with you. They are like the pop-ups when you are searching the Internet. Whenever you log on, there they are. Your ship is sailing and they want to hitch themselves a ride. The baggage they bring on board, however, can be damaging to your journey. You may find yourself inheriting not only them but the enemies they have and whatever drama comes along with them. As a consequence you may find yourself involved in things that you have no knowledge of and your own influence tarnished.

One challenge of success will be the labels others will want to place on you. Like the stamps the post office puts on mail—"priority," "first class," and so on—people like to slap labels on other people, so they can categorize you for easy handling. People want to categorize you based on something they are already familiar with. These labels can stick no matter how biased or untrue they may be. You will want to do all you can to be sure you control what is said about you, your reputation and your name, your message and your mission.

Racial, social, sexual, and political labels are often placed on people, but rarely do they accurately describe who we really are. Just as a zip code can't predict a person's education level or credit rating, labels don't necessarily depict a person's true nature. Still, many of us are guilty by association, even if the association is a brief and nonmeaningful one. Unfortunately, there is not much we can do about people who insist on labeling people based on associations and incomplete information, so it is up to you to be careful of the people with whom you associate and make sure the label on your package is the one you want people to see.

27

Think Interdependence, Not Independence

Striving to better ourselves is a good thing, but it doesn't have to be at the expense of those who love us. Our connection to one another is what makes each of us strong as individuals. As we make our own way in the world, many of us turn away from our family connections, focusing on building careers and new lives for ourselves. But cutting family ties may actually hurt our chances for success. In order to thrive, we need support and encouragement from the people who know and love us. We can be successful and connected to our past, not letting it run our lives, but rather allowing it to inform them.

True, family members may not understand your new world. Then, however, it is up to you to share your life and experiences so they have a better idea of what you do and where you are trying to go. No matter how many degrees you earn or the list of accomplishments on your resume, some things about you will never change. When your career is over and you look to retire, you will want a place to retreat where people are supportive and happy to see you. Here are ways to make sure you stay grounded while you also soar as high as you can.

- Maintain family traditions. Some of our best memories from childhood include family dinners, annual trips, and other traditions. Whenever you can, work to maintain these customs, as they will be times you look back on and cherish as you mature. Certainly, traveling home for the holidays and other special events involves precious time and can be very expensive. But it's important to make the effort if your schedule permits. Just think about the gift you are giving your children and how happy you will make your own parents, grandparents, and other relatives, who've known you since you were a child.

- Face the past and move forward. Not all family situations are like television's *The Cosby Show*. For many of us, visits back home mean pain and discomfort. If there is something in your family's past that causes you stress, be truthful with yourself and your family about your feelings. Sometimes the best thing we can do for ourselves and others is to excuse ourselves from family gatherings for a while in order to get therapy or counseling to help us face our issues and the things that have happened to us. Or perhaps you need to summon up the courage to sit down and have a serious but necessary talk with the family member you feel hurt you. This is not about arguing, screaming, or fighting, it's about healthy closure and moving forward, which is usually a great relief for everyone involved.

- Start new traditions. Families come in many forms; sometimes they are made up of blood relatives and other times they include a collection of close friends. No matter who makes up your family, you can create ways to celebrate life in a new way that is completely free of any issues from the past. Resurrect the tradition of Sunday dinner. Come up with a new way to observe the Sabbath as a family; start a new New Year's or Fourth of July tradition. Infuse them with your personality and make them your own.

- Thank those who have supported you in your success. No one makes it to the top on their own. If you think about it, there are people who've been there for you all the way, those who planted the first seeds of success in your brain many years ago. Why not display and use pictures, jewelry, or other mementos that depict special times or special moments from your past and incorporate them into your present life.

- Share family stories with your children. Whether it's the children in your own family or young people whom you mentor at church or through volunteer activities, it is important to share your family's history with the generation coming next. Organize family photos into albums, or transfer them to CDs for safekeeping. Even consider writing down particularly interesting or important stories so they aren't forgotten. It helps youngsters know who they are and the rich tradition from which they came.

- Bless your family time. Making time to connect with your family on a regular basis will add more meaning to your life. And don't just be there in body; bring your spirit and intention with you. The people you love deserve your true and undivided attention, whether you're setting aside time to share a DVD and popcorn together or maintaining the tradition of midnight mass. Create sacred time that you and your family spend together. You will strengthen ties to last a lifetime.

- Celebrate your successes with your family. Everyone likes to belong. And many of us learn that achieving success often makes those around us a bit uncomfortable. People remember you for who you were and don't necessarily accept who you've become. At the same time some people who achieve a level of success shrink from their achievements, fearing that their family may see them as full of themselves. Moms and dads, and grandmas and grandpas think just about everything you do is pretty amazing. No matter how old you are, they still see you as their "baby" who can do no wrong. Share the news about the new funder you secured or the scores from your certification exam. Your loved ones may not even know exactly what they are celebrating, but they will cheer you on all the same.

28

Build Your Dream Team

To make an important choice, we know the steps involved: we gather information so that we can make informed decisions and we take responsibility for what we are doing. Then we clean out the junk in our trunk: the negative thoughts, the old hurts and bitterness, and anything else that is standing between us and our dream. Our next step is to build a dream team who can assist us in making decisions and support us along the way.

No one makes it alone. We can't know everything, be everything, or do everything. Consider a professional football team. There is so much more to the team than just the players we see on the field on Sunday afternoon. There are scouts, for example, who attend college games to identify potential new players. They look for talent, skill, and potential to fit their pro team rosters. They sometimes start following these players long before they are even eligible to play pro ball. These scouts envision how these players might fit in, not on their current teams, but on the teams of the future. That's how Super Bowl teams are built.

For the coach, as for any leader, personnel considerations are among the keys to success. The team's athletes are his assets, defined by their positions, and put together according to NFL rules within the team's budget. Some positions represent more valuable assets than others. Few pro football teams can perform without a talented quarterback. The same is true of a CEO of a Fortune 500 firm, or the senior partner at a law firm. All down the line, personnel considerations are key. A business leader's team is put in place by the human resources department that recruits and trains top talent. Like the NFL scouts, an HR professional is the core of a strong organization. And just as the players execute a winning season, the CEO's talented employees work to build a strong infrastructure and expand the company's selling markets, offering shareholders and investors a positive return on their investment.

Parents need a team at home as well. Mothers and fathers teach their children about responsibility and teamwork by assigning them chores that help the household run smoothly. Tasks like washing the dishes, making their beds, emptying the trash all work together to help Mom and Dad balance their workload and family obligations. Smart parents know that in order to have a smoothly running home, the entire family has to pitch in.

As the CEO of your own team, you must build a strong team of people around you in order to see your dream become a reality. You're in charge and will guide your team to success. But it is your team who will execute their responsibilities with passion and commitment.

29

Know Who's Who in Your Life

Nearly all the key relationships in your life can be broken down into three categories: confidants, constituents, and comrades. One key to a good life is knowing who among those around you falls into which group.

Confidants are those whose relationships with you are lifelong. These are people who love you unconditionally. These people will stand by you and have your back in good times and bad. Your best interest is their number one priority. These relationships are rare and typically require years of nurturing to solidify the trust.

These people are literally your confidants. If you don't have trust in them, then you can't openly express yourself, share your feelings, or seek their counsel. Sharing too much with the wrong people can have disastrous consequences. True confidants never seek to use what they know about us for their own gain or ever throw our secrets back in our face. The number of people who should be your confidants is very small.

Constituents are in your life walking alongside you, and they have the same goals, values, and principles you have. They may be business associates or church members, people who have similar goals and aspirations. But they are not confidants and aren't always there for you. They may share a desire for common outcomes, but your best interest is not their main concern. When you no longer share common goals or you don't serve their purpose, they are out the door to find someone who does.

Constituents are important, though. They can contribute energy, passion, and enthusiasm to your goals. But you can't expect them to love you unconditionally or even have your best interest at heart. They may differ from you in significant ways, including background and culture. While you may have different backgrounds, social interests, career paths, or departments, you share common values that bring you together. Work with constituents to accomplish common goals and build bridges. Just be sure not to expect constituents to have the loyalty of confidants. Like some friendships, constituents are typically seasonal relationships. They are with you for a reason and when the season is up, they move on.

Comrades don't necessarily even share your goals,

values, or principles, nor do they care much about the issues that are important to you, as do constituents. They are not for you unconditionally like confidants. In fact, they can have more in common with your enemies than they do with you. They are attracted to you because you are against what they are against. They may not get to know or even like you, but on the field of battle they join together with you as soldiers to defeat a common enemy. Once the fight is over, the relationship ends or at least cools. Your only bond is a common enemy.

30

Determine How Your Affiliations Will Feed You

The more successful you become, the more you'll be approached about participating in or joining various groups and causes. Before you say yes, you will need to answer some questions for yourself. You'll need to decide in what ways you can offer the most significant and positive contribution to the group. And you need to assess what contribution the group can make to you. Managing expectations about your association with any group is critical to a positive experience both for you and for the organization.

You may be seeking ways to advance your career. So you ask yourself if there are people involved with the organization that you want to meet. If you are looking to join a church, ask yourself if it is one that you believe will feed you spiritually. The point is that if you aren't being fed in some way by your association with a particular organization, then you won't likely remain committed to it. There will be no passion in your involvement, and your membership will become just another box to check off on your to-do list.

Ask yourself what you can contribute that is unique and valuable. What important talents can you offer that no one else can? Whether because of your passion for the cause or some special skills you can contribute, you could become irreplaceable to an organization. But if you cannot add something new to the organization, it is probably not the right choice for you.

If you're already committed, do a review of all your affiliations to make sure your time and efforts are being spent wisely. List each club, organization, and committee to which you belong. Include sororities, church groups, volunteer activities, work committees, political campaigns, choirs, tennis teams, co-op boards—everything. Then assess your level of commitment for each one from none to high. Now write down how you feel about being associated with each group. Take steps to terminate any association with groups where your commitment and feelings are not positive. Letting go of groups that are not feeding you will not only free up your time but make you feel less weighed down. If you don't feel fed by your current church, it doesn't make sense to continue to attend services there. If your kids are in college, why are you still serving on the PTA?

Set clear boundaries for your involvement with the groups that remain. If you agreed to stuff envelopes with flyers about an event one weekend, don't let that turn into your organizing the event, unless that is something you really want to do.

31

Appreciate the Beauty of Your Patchwork Heritage

I love quilts—stray pieces of fabric that are no longer useful by themselves put together with other remnants that then become a cover that warms and protects us from the damp and cold. Grandpa's flannel pajamas end up connected to Grandma's Christmas apron and Auntie's favorite dress. A family is much like a quilt. It can't exist without the contributions of many people, who bring their unique qualities to the whole. Just as the fabrics in a quilt vary in color and texture, so the members of a family differ in personality and style.

The top of a quilt may be beautiful and neatly constructed, but turn a quilt over and the underside reveals disparate stitching patterns, stray threads, and a variety of knots. Families have an underside too, and perhaps a past that, like the quilt, may include a few less-than-even stitches. But that is normal.

As you grow more successful and develop new relationships, the underside of your family may become more and more distracting and disturbing to you. You may be tempted to compare your family to the other, more accomplished people in your life and find fault. You may also assume that the undersides of your associates' family quilts look neater and tidier than yours.

That's the time to remind yourself that there is one important ingredient in making a family, and that's love. We don't get to choose the families we are born into, but love is what makes families beautiful. So don't let your newfound shiny life blind you to the beauty of your own quilt. Don't let success lead you to keep your quilt hidden away in a box under the bed.

While we are each different, love and forgiveness are the core to every strong family. And no matter how successful we get or how independent we may seem, we need people in our lives who know us and know where we come from. We all crave belonging, unity with people who know and love us. We don't have to agree with or relate to each other on every issue, but we all want and need to love and be loved.

The quilt of your ancestors represents all of who you are; good and not so good, it is what makes you unique.

Use it to shield you from the cold that life sometimes brings, to comfort you, to sustain you when you need to be reminded of who you are and where you came from. Add your own fabric patches and pass it on to the next generation, who will benefit from your contributions.

32

R-E-S-P-E-C-T Differences
and Celebrate Diversity

All human beings gravitate to like individuals and avoid those who are different. We feel more comfortable around people who have perceived commonalities—shared culture, profession, age, belief system. We like to hang with people with whom we can immediately relate and confirm our values and opinions.

We go out into the world, to our jobs, schools, or other daytime activities, and interact with people of all kinds. But the moment the whistle blows or the school bell rings, we retreat to our segregated neighborhoods, churches, and social groups to interact with "our own kind."

Differences challenge us. When someone is not like us, we are curious and may even feel threatened or intimidated. Those insecurities can keep us from reaching out to people and cut us off from the opportunities to learn and grow as people.

Jesus interacted with everyone, the Samaritan woman at the well, Zacchaeus the tax collector, and the lepers, all individuals shunned by society. He did not associate himself with any exclusionary cliques; he showed love to all people. We must learn to do the same.

We can learn to share our views and discuss our divergent opinions without being disrespectful. We can replace the urge to bring down those who think differently with a genuine desire to agree to disagree with goodwill.

Discovering where your ideas and views intersect with others is more important than standing on either side of the line of discussion, arguing that you are "in the right."

We can all do better at managing our differences if we spend time getting to know and understand people outside our immediate circles. In fact, people are more the same than they are different. No matter what our skin color, our political affiliation, or our religious beliefs, our concerns are essentially identical. We all want to provide for ourselves and our families, be good citizens of our communities, and live with as much meaning and joy as possible.

If all the people around you look exactly like you, vote

the way you vote, and think just like you do, your view of the world becomes very small and unbalanced. Differences are easy to spot, but it requires a truly secure and open person to look deep into another person to find common ground.

—

Money
Money
Money

33

Success Is About
More Than Finances

When my wife and I sold our house a few years ago, our profits were nearly double the purchase price. I looked hard to find another home in a great neighborhood that would offer the same kind of return on investment if we decided to sell again. I found a great house and shared my plan to buy it with my family and close friends. But one friend gave me some surprising advice. He told me not to buy it!

He could hear in my voice that I was trying to convince myself that the house was a great deal, and it was. The only problem was I didn't like the house! I liked the deal, but the house, not so much. Focusing on the money and ignoring the fact that the house didn't feel all that comfortable to me, that I couldn't really picture me, my wife, or my family there—that was the source of the hesitation that my friend picked up on. In the end, I opted not to buy it, because my feelings were too strong to ignore. Buying the house would have been a mistake. I would have acted solely on the finances and ignored other, internal factors, such as the unhappiness of actually living there.

I eventually looked at nearly thirty homes before I decided to purchase one that, in addition to meeting all my financial requirements, was also one that I liked very much and for which I would feel good about spending years writing checks for the mortgage.

We often make decisions, whether it's buying a house, taking a job, or entering into a relationship, because they look good on paper. We have all likely dated someone who had all the characteristics we look for in a mate—honesty, integrity, faith in God, beautiful eyes and lovely smile, and so on. But no matter how great potential partners may look and act, if we don't feel a deep connection to them as people, if we don't like them and respect them as human beings, then no matter how great their characteristics line up on paper, the relationship is doomed.

Our pursuit of success sometimes causes us to lose touch with what's at the core of why we are working so hard in the first place. The singular quest to attain a high level of success is often the reason many people forget to place the same emphasis on what's in their soul and heart. I am not suggesting that anything is wrong with pursuing goals, financial or otherwise. Take pleasure in the deal. Just be careful not to get caught up in the belief that the only measure of success is money.

Pursue that which nurtures your inner life. Whether you're a Wall Street executive who sings in the church choir, a communications executive who writes fiction on the weekends, or a small business owner who serves on a nonprofit board, make time for the Creator and the things that bring you joy.

34

Know What Your Money
Is Worth

People who were happy when they bought their clothes at the thrift store typically remain happy once they can afford designer duds. Those who weren't are still the same unhappy people they were when they were poor, they just dress better.

Learning how to be satisfied and content with what you have and to feel grateful for it starts with understanding what money can and cannot do. There are things in life that you can't put a price on. Things like having a family that loves and adores you, the support of a friendship that has lasted for many years, the wonderful feeling of accomplishment that comes from working hard and finally seeing your effort pay off: you cannot value these "possessions" in dollars.

I've read countless books about the lives of famous CEOs, actors, athletes, and even spiritual leaders. Almost all share that their great accomplishment and wealth were born out of struggle. God offers us the magnificent beauty of life absolutely free. If you think you don't have anything to be grateful for, consider the way the light hits the trees at sunset, the beautiful white puffy clouds against a majestic blue sky, the sound of a child's laughter, the crash of the ocean as the waves meet the shore, the unconditional greeting we receive each day from our favorite pet, or the warmth of sunshine on our face, and I could go on and on. We have to learn to count these fee-free blessings among our personal assets. I once went on a cruise through Alaska and saw polar bears playing happily, diving over and over into the frigid waters without a thought of us tourists watching from our luxury liner. The bears were aware that the true beauty of Alaska was in the water where they were, not on the deck of our cruise ship.

The things that truly matter in life—the cool touch of a mother's hand on the forehead of a child with a fever, the hug of a friend you have been separated from for a long time, the excitement of rounding home base in the neighborhood kickball game—these are the things that have nothing to do with tax deductions or 401(k)s or stocks and bonds, but everything to do with what life is about. They are the list of your personal spiritual assets.

Without these assets you are in spiritual default. These items cannot be deducted. They are priceless and have nothing to do with shares or profits. When you add up everything in life, the best things are free. If you are personally and spiritually bankrupt, having capital gains means nothing at all.

If you are not happy with your financial situation, you will need to take steps to change it. But before you do anything about ridding yourself of debt or saving for a home, conduct an audit of your personal spiritual assets. Enjoying the spoils of success can be exhilarating. But remember to appreciate the beauty of life as well; it's free, but it will fill you up in a way that money and things never will.

35

Money Buys You Options

Consider the difference between flying coach and first-class. If you buy the coach, supersaver ticket, your options are limited in terms of the date you can fly, the time you can travel, and what seat you sit in. Your best bet for food is a bag of chips or nuts, and don't even think about comfort. If you're lucky, the person in the row ahead of you won't recline their seat into your lap.

Now contrast that with sitting in first class. You pay more for your seat than in coach, sometimes a lot more. But in return for that higher fare, you can fly anytime you want, on just about any day, and once you've enjoyed the hot towels and complimentary drinks and delicious food, and have topped off the meal with warm cookies, you can recline your seat back as far as you wish. There is so much room between your seats that the passenger in the row behind you could care less!

Money gives you options for where you live, what you wear, and so on. Without it, you have few choices or maybe no choice at all. The math is simple: the more money you have, the more options you have.

But money won't make your journey through life any happier. With money, life is just easier to navigate; you feel more secure and aren't worried about how you'll get through the day. When you feel secure, you are free to pay attention to other things that can help you expand your life even further. Whether it's pursuing a hobby or another degree, upgrading your home, or investing in a new business, having money allows you to step out and pursue a life over and above just getting by. If your finances are not what you'd like them to be, do what you need to do to improve your situation.

36

Be the Master of Your Debt

Good credit is the foundation for establishing your future buying power.

While so much has been in the news recently about the level of debt we carry, debt itself is not necessarily a bad thing. Whether we use it to buy our dream house, a nice automobile to replace the car that breaks down constantly, or a much-anticipated exotic vacation, when we handle debt in a responsible manner, it can afford us the opportunity to make more easily the large purchases that can truly enhance our lives.

Nothing is wrong with wanting a new Mercedes or a vacation home. We work hard for our money and want nice things. The problems come when we put the acquisition of these items ahead of the people in our lives.

No matter how many diamonds you buy, they will never offer you love, friendship, or peace from within.

People spend years working extra hours, away from family and friends, missing important milestones in the lives of their children. They put family aside to attend meetings and events that will lead to more money and more things. They may end up with all the things they want only to realize they are still missing internal peace.

If you misuse debt, you experience sadness and anxiety each month as you pull the envelope from the mailbox with the credit card bill that says you've spent more than you can afford. One of the inevitable and unexpected challenges of life pops up—the car needs a new transmission, a medical procedure is not covered by insurance, or the hot water heater goes on the fritz—and you find yourself short on funds. The things we buy don't just cost us money; there are other, less tangible costs as well. In order to stay on top of the amount but continue to live, we throw good money after bad debt, taking out interest-only loans, no-down-payment financing, and other seemingly "easy" financing options. Like a juggler in the circus, we keep the plates in the air by making the minimum payments, just getting by for yet another month.

Eventually, however, we get tired of trying to keep the plates aloft. We take our eye off the task of keeping up, and soon one or more of the plates are crashing to the ground. We have to borrow money to stay afloat; we spend sleepless nights wondering how we will keep up with paying for the things we bought. Our shame and embarrassment only compounds the situation, as we hide the reality of our financial problems from others, working to put on a good face to the rest of the world, essentially cutting ourselves off from the help we so desperately need. The worst part of this situation is that we are now stuck in worry and despair, unable to move forward financially or any other way.

The way out of this scenario is not to win the lottery or otherwise suddenly get rich. The answer is to begin to approach our finances with respect and learn to control our resources, opportunities, and most importantly, the emotions that led us into this situation. Our emotions, our lack of a sense of self-worth, led us to purchase items we couldn't afford in order to fill some unnamed hole within. To become truly rich, we must begin at this place within.

Identify Your Personal
Financial Buzzwords

Describe how you feel about words like *spend, save, bud-get, luxury,* and *discounted.* What emotions and feelings come up for you? Do you feel ashamed, anxious, upset, happy, excited, or angry? These are clues that will help you understand any emotional baggage you may have associated with money. Once you are aware of the effect of these trigger words, it is easier to understand why you approach money the way you do. Knowing your financial buzzwords can help you handle money in a more responsible and balanced way, whether your issue is overspending or keeping a bit too tight a grip on every nickel.

Sit down and map out where you want to be in the short term as well as in the long term. Short-term goals might include replacing the hot water heater or taking an overnight trip to see your parents. Long-term goals could be buying a home or a second car or pursuing a higher degree. Having these goals and a budget in place to reach them will help the spender pass up the great sale on fishing poles when there are two perfectly good ones in the garage, and it will help the saver agree to spend a little money on a night out knowing that the bills are paid and the money for the future has been added to the investment accounts for the month.

Controlling our use of credit cards often requires a totally new way of thinking about our lives and talking about finances. Of course it is important for us to learn and understand the basics of finance and to become familiar with terms such as *interest rates* and *APR*.

If you are part of a couple and share the job of the family's finances, you must also learn your partner's financial language. Arguments over money are common among couples whose financial agendas differ. He is a spender, feeling that he has reached a place in life where money should be of no concern. If he wants it, he buys it. She is a saver, feeling that money is best put away for a rainy day, and she counts each and every penny. To her, money is for saving, to prepare for the future, and she sees his spending habits as irresponsible and shortsighted. To him, money is for spending, to buy things to enjoy life, and he sees her as a miser with no desire for fun and spontaneity. They are each speaking a different money language, and as a result, they never see eye to eye when discussing their finances.

This couple needs a new financial vocabulary. They need to agree on words that will describe her need to save and his need to spend, to the understanding and satisfaction of the other. Neither saving nor spending needs to have a negative meaning. What is required is communication and discussion about what is important to each partner, the merits of their respective financial views, and then a meeting of the minds where he, the spender, recognizes the merits of a financial strategy that not only affords fun but plans for the future, and where she, the saver, sees the merits in spending to add a bit of fun to life, as well as putting a budget in place for tomorrow.

Getting to this place of responsible use of money is not just about avoiding credit cards. Debit cards, while seemingly the answer to out-of-control credit card use, can cause difficulty as well if not used in conjunction with a budget. While they keep you from getting the month-end credit card bill that you can't afford to pay, if you purchase a new flat-screen television with a debit card but then don't have the cash to pay the rent at the end of the month, you are still not exhibiting healthy spending habits. If you have issues with overspending using credit cards, then using a debit card as part of a well-thought-out spending plan can certainly help, not to mention the added convenience it offers. But your spending must still be in line with your budget and existing bills. No matter what kind of card you are using, spend within your budget, keep track of what you buy, balance your accounts at the end of each month, and communicate clearly about money in language that decodes your attitudes about money. You will be on your way to financial freedom now and in the future.

38

Recognize the
Stewardship of Success

Leadership = influence. That's what my friend John Maxwell, the bestselling author and leadership guru, teaches. Following his thinking, prosperity then has a measure of influence as well. The people around us define our level of influence, our power base. Influence is hard to hide. People recognize influence; they crave it, whether it's yours or their own. When you have influence, you want to use it, and when others see that you have it, they want to find ways to use it too, in negative and positive ways. At work, if you have influence with your boss, others may try to get you to make their case for them. If you have influence with a certain official, for example, people may try to get you to advance their cause. The challenge is how to maintain influence without its being tainted, especially by those who want to use your power for their own gain without regard for yours.

Who speaks for you and to you? The answers to these

questions are important because whoever they are can either lift you up or bring you down. Someone may have their own agenda and may borrow your message and claim to speak for you for their own gain.

It is not uncommon for others to speak for us, though. A child who takes a note from home to a schoolteacher is speaking on behalf of the parent who wrote it. Those in senior management positions have middle management teams that speak for them to the staff at large, to customers, and to the general public. There is no way to avoid having people speak on your behalf. We must be careful, though, who we trust to be our spokesperson and for what purpose.

It's like when you have an accountant or some other financial professional prepare your annual tax return. You have hired this person to speak on your behalf to the IRS. Or if you have ever had to hire an attorney to represent you in a legal issue, or a real estate agent to buy or sell a home or other property, they are speaking for you. If they are competent and professional, then you can be reasonably sure they are speaking for you with success, but if they are not, you may be in trouble.

Your challenge will be to find competent, professional people who represent you as you would want them to. They are key to your stewardship of success!

39

Leave a Legacy of Wealth

God bestowed wealth upon the Hebrews, who went from suffering to success. After the Hebrews were enslaved for over four hundred years, the Egyptians handed over to them the wealth of Egypt (Exodus 3:21–22, KJV).

Taking responsible care of your finances is a way not just to build a stable foundation for yourself but also to create a legacy of wealth to pass along to your children and eventually your grandchildren. This does not mean that you need to leave your children a substantial trust fund, while I am sure they would certainly not mind if you did! I am talking about setting the example of sound financial habits. The knowledge of how to manage their money is one of the best gifts you can give your children.

While few of us inherited an estate or a substantial stock account from our parents, passing along the foundation for a financial future to your children will help them avoid some of the money mistakes you may have made.

God loves to redeem us, allowing us to regain what we have lost, even in some cases squandered. Just as in the Bible story of the Hebrews and Egyptians, the blessings we receive don't always come from nice people in our life. Consider the wildly successful companies sometimes funded by dishonest people. It is always God who blesses us, not people. People are simply the instruments God uses to illuminate his greater purpose. Rest in God, and you will never find yourself empty-handed. Anything that isn't fruitful or profitable is not of God. Like the fruit from the tree once the growth cycle is complete, profit is what is left when the transaction is complete. God commands that in whatever you do, something must be left.

Teaching your children about the true value of blessings and how to manage their finances is positioning them to succeed in their own lives.

40

Realistic Home Buying

Buying a home is almost a rite of passage in achieving success.

The first hurdle is financial. When you are considering buying a home, you must be preapproved for a mortgage. Your next step is to consider what kind of loan is best for you.

Then the fun part: you can go out and look at the available houses. According to most real estate agents, buying a home is about making a series of compromises. You must first determine your must-haves. Then you have to decide what you would like but could live without.

If you know for sure you must have two bathrooms in order for your growing family to get out of the house on time in the morning, or lots of sunlight to sit and read, or windowsills for your budding plant collection, and a kitchen large enough for you to cook gourmet meals in and hang out together in as a family, then stand firm when working with a real estate agent or searching for your new home on the Internet. Don't overlook foreclosures and short sales, as they sometimes offer incredible deals on amazing properties.

VISION

Consider two important things when house hunting. Try to look past the current appearance. Despite the seller's furniture and decorating style, imagine the house filled with your personal items. Can you see your favorite colors and design style there? The kind of furniture that you like and the fabrics and textures that you love? Let your imagination run wild; mentally redecorate the rooms, move walls, add new hardware and fixtures. Every diamond begins as an unpolished stone.

Second, honor your first impression. Author Malcolm Gladwell says our "blink" reaction is always dead-on accurate. If you have a bad feeling about something, that is your God-given inner voice telling you *No!* If you walk into a house and have a bad feeling, it doesn't matter how beautiful the bamboo wood floors and the stainless steel appliances are, you can be sure you won't be happy there.

At the same time, even if you have a great feeling

about a home, you shouldn't underestimate the work and cost that goes into repairing or renovating. A house where the entire heating system has to be modernized, or whose plumbing needs to be replaced, will need more than a good feeling to bring it up to par. When looking for a home, you will need to balance your vision with reality. Buying a house and moving are both on the list of life's most stressful events. You may want to make some improvements to put your signature on a house—and often these will help increase your selling value—but you won't likely have the energy or the finances to immediately jump into a major remodeling project as soon as you move in. So proceed with great caution.

TIMING

It is impossible to control the inventory of available homes once you start looking. But you should be aware of your own timing requirements and where you will need flexibility. If you have to wait until after the school year is complete before you can move your family from one coast to another, then short-sale opportunities (where you quickly buy a house from a bank or other lending institution) are probably not an option for you. If you have lost your job or taken some other major financial hit, you may have to make significant compromises since you won't be able to afford to hold out for the house that meets all the requirements on your list.

The seller will sometimes work with you to offer a schedule that meets both your needs. They could rent the home from you after the closing until they move out and you are ready to move in. Or you may rent a temporary place for you and your family while you are between homes. Clearly expressing your needs and looking to come up with creative solutions will create a winning situation for both of you. Also be sure to allow time for an inspection and an appraisal, usually required by your lender. You should never purchase a home without them, as you want to be sure there are no hidden issues and that the property is appropriately valued.

The final aspect of timing is trying to avoid what my wife calls "the perfect dress" syndrome. She says that many ladies go out and shop for the perfect dress. Whether it's for a party, wedding, or other event, she will often find the right dress—perfect color, style, and size— at the first shop she visits. But she doesn't buy it. Instead, she visits other stores, trying on many more dresses, before she goes back to get the very first dress, at the very first store she went to. And it's not just the ladies who shop this way. I know plenty of men who buy their suits and ties in the same way. With our consumer-obsessed culture, we have so many options from which to choose that sometimes making a choice becomes extremely difficult even when you know in your heart that you have already seen exactly what you want. You wonder if a better option could be waiting in the store across the street. The same principle can be applied to shopping for a house. Just be careful that you don't lose out on a great house because you spent too much time shopping for something better. When you know, you know. Don't wait. Put in an offer, and rest in the comfort of knowing you found the house you were looking for.

Mindfully Relate and Mate

41

The R&D Before the Relationship

You wouldn't likely consider taking a medication that hadn't been studied, tested, and FDA-approved. Few of us would allow our child to take a pill without knowing everything we could learn about it. We wouldn't buy a car from someone we didn't know or one that we hadn't test-driven. Yet many of us mindlessly enter into something as important as a relationship with little thought to the fundamental requirements we need to be happy.

Whenever I find myself shopping in one of the big retail box stores, I am always blown away by the number of products and choices on the shelves. From meat to toilet paper to flat-screen televisions, there seem to be countless versions of every product. I often wonder how businesses decide the product specs for the forty-eight varieties of blue cheese salad dressing on the shelf.

Perhaps you've wondered the same thing. Say you installed some beautiful, shiny new granite countertops in your kitchen, and you need a product that will clean them without scratching. Then as if by magic, you are wheeling your cart down through the store and the exact cleanser appears in the cleaning product aisle. And you think, *Who determined that the product I needed should be made?*

Or have you ever asked yourself why some of the medicines we have to take are so incredibly expensive? I have had prescriptions for pills, some of which have cost up to $100. To make matters worse, my insurance didn't cover the costs and I had to pay for the medication out of pocket. How could such a tiny little white pill be so costly?

New products on the market are the result of research and development (or R&D) departments. Companies consider R&D fundamental to their success. R&D departments study their target consumers, their habits and preferences, in terms of where and when they shop. They conduct focus groups asking customers what they can improve about old products and what they want in new products. And they help decide the new trends so the company can stay ahead of the curve. Pharmaceutical companies spend billions of dollars developing new drugs. It can take years to create new treatments, and the testing as well as the federal approval process is long and costly. The cost of this process is factored into the consumer's price.

Research and development is critical in our personal lives as well, especially when it comes to our relationships. Do you do the necessary amount of R&D, reviewing the character of a potential mate to make sure they are who they seem to be? Do you conduct compatibility tests to ensure this is someone you want to spend your life with? Do you apply the research you've done in the past, taking what you've learned and applying it to potential new relationships?

Of course we wouldn't go about asking the critical questions of a potential mate on our first date, but we are wise to spend the necessary time to make sure we know the person we're with before our desires take us down a path to a place we don't want to be.

Just as you wouldn't leave your child with a babysitter whose background and experience you didn't trust, don't turn over your heart to someone before you determine who they are, what they want, what they stand for, and what they believe in. We are often afraid we may offend people by asking certain questions. But if you find yourself afraid, and use that fear as an excuse not to ask, then your message to the other person is that you will take them on any terms.

Entering into a relationship without securing important data about the other person is like driving down the road wearing a blindfold—self-imposed sightlessness. Blindness leaves us very vulnerable. Yet I see people every day getting married to people whom they have little real knowledge of. When they finally get up the nerve to ask the questions they should have asked during courtship, they are already married and in the middle of drama and crisis. Both parties may have entered the marriage with the best of intentions, but they still find themselves in deep regret.

If you've done this, luckily for you, Jesus, according to the Bible, healed blindness more than any other affliction. If you've made this mistake in the past, vow to walk forward in that knowledge and approach your next potential partnership differently. Put on your lab coat, get out your clipboard and microscope, and get to researching.

42

The Confidence Factor

Few things are more off-putting on a first date than someone who appears desperate. In our quest to be clear about what we want and need from a mate, many people discuss their desire to be married on the first or second date.

While you may not want to waste time with someone who isn't serious about the future, which I certainly understand, talking about wanting to marry someone you just met does not put you in a position of strength. A man looks to marry a woman who loves him, not a woman in love with the idea of getting married, much less a woman who is desperate.

While "You complete me," the famous line Tom Cruise delivered in the movie *Jerry Maguire,* seems romantic, in real life it's really oversentimental and immature. No human being can or should "complete" another person.

Only God can do that for us. Many people get married to share expenses or to raise children, but when financial situations change, and children grow up and leave home, there's nothing keeping the pair together. When you are considering entering into a lifelong commitment like marriage, you have to decide if you want to be with this person in holistic terms or settle for someone simply to satisfy only part of your needs.

Sometimes we get so focused on the other person and what they need that we give little consideration to what they offer us. We refer to them as partners or lovers, but the truth is they are takers. Lust and self-gratification are focused inward. Love is about the other person and what you can contribute to their life. It is impossible to be a desperate giver, but it is easy to be a desperate taker.

We are each created in God's complete and divine image, be confident in that fact. There is a misconception that marriage is fifty-fifty. In fact, it is a one hundred–one hundred deal. It demands that both parties bring one hundred percent of who they are and what they offer to the relationship. It is complement, not completement that results in a successful marriage. We should work to enhance each other's strengths, not compensate for someone else's weaknesses. A marriage is a union that brings together two individuals who are already strong and who are together even stronger.

If you've ever been the desperate one in a relationship, you likely already know that you were not at your best emotionally, or any other way for that matter. You probably called too much, incessantly texted and emailed them; you thought about them all day long, wondering where they were, what they were doing, and when you would see them next. You stopped calling your friends, gave up your interests, and dropped everything whenever they called. If your partner was happy, so were you. If they wanted to go out or stay in, so did you. Your identity as an individual was replaced by your identity as part of a couple, and nothing else in your life—not your job, your family, or your friends—mattered.

If you've been there, you know that for someone to act as though they have no life of their own and make you the center of their existence is a serious red flag suggesting that your intended may have some significant holes in their life. They likely have a serious lack of self-esteem that they will want you to fill. Ignoring these signs and entering blindly into a relationship with someone like this is not only a bad idea, it can eventually become very dangerous.

43

Recognize Relationship Deal Breakers

Love is about giving. Love looks to truly connect with another person and wonders what it can do to support them and contribute to their well-being. If your relationships seem flat and unfulfilling, if you have difficulty communicating, if you cynically think that everyone who approaches you has ulterior motives and will ultimately betray you, then you may need to consider whether you are standing in the way of finding true love in your life. Love requires hope; it requires openness and willingness to risk. We mistakenly think that love is about what we get, but the truth is it is about sharing, enriching another, and finding your joy in that process.

We are all made in God's likeness and as such deserve good, honest, supportive love that helps build us up, not tear us down. If you don't feel safe, physically or emotionally, in a relationship, then you are not loved, and it's vital that you remove yourself from the situation.

Physical and emotional violence should be on everyone's list of deal breakers, no matter who you are. If you see signs of manipulation, psychological game playing, and attempts at control in the beginning, you can rest assured that as the relationship progresses, these issues will only escalate. The person who is occasionally critical in the beginning of a relationship often later becomes the giver of angry and unwanted feedback regarding everything you do. Before entering into a relationship, know the personality traits and behaviors that you are compatible with. People can be polar opposites in terms of how they think and act, but if they have respect and effective communication, they can make things work.

Domestic abuse affects people of all classes, colors, ages, sexes, and religions. No one should ever threaten to or actually put their hands on you in a malicious or violent way. No relationship is worth your emotional health or your physical safety. Love gives; it provides a secure place where two people can grow together and commit to serving one another. Physical or emotional injury should never factor into the equation.

There are other deal breakers to consider, including addiction. This is not to say that if your partner develops an addiction, you should automatically leave the relationship. But you should seek help and support. You need to decide how much you are willing to take on in order to save your union. There is no prize for being a martyr. If you grew up in a home where your father or mother was an alcoholic, then you may need to know if your loved one is committed to getting treatment before you decide to stay. If your loved one is not willing to share in the responsibilities of caring for your home and children, even though you both have demanding full-time jobs outside the home, then you have to decide if you can have a serious relationship with a person who feels this way.

It is up to you to decide what you require to have a healthy relationship. To me it is tragic to see so many people who know what they should do but are so afraid of being alone, or risking their heart, that they don't act. When you are sure when to stay and fight, when to leave, and when to wait and see, you will find the love that you desire, whether it is in your current relationship or not.

44

Choose a Mate for You, Not Your Profession

Everyone assumed because I was a pastor that I would marry someone who was gifted musically, played an instrument, and perhaps led the church choir. The woman who became my wife loves music and has a gorgeous voice, but she does not play an instrument, does not like to perform, and has no interest in leading anyone's choir. Several friends cautioned me to think twice before marrying her because they didn't believe she could add value to my work as a minister. Now I had to ask myself, did I want to marry a woman who fit my profession or my personhood? I came to the conclusion that it would not matter if my wife could sing like Aretha if we couldn't communicate, share the same values and dreams, and love and support one another. We might share a platform, but we wouldn't see eye to eye.

I've counseled many professional athletes and movie

stars who find themselves in the midst of marriage struggles once their time on the court or the screen was over. Things were fine when life meant time on the red carpet and all they needed was a beautiful partner on their arm or cheering them from the sidelines. But after the limelight had faded away, and life became less about who they were wearing or the next charity event they'd attend, they found there was nothing holding their relationship together.

When mates are chosen as if in a casting call for a beauty pageant, the relationship lacks substance. Shopping for a watch, we chose one based on how it looks and assume, since it's a watch, that it will keep perfect time. You can't, however, choose a partner this way. When the inevitable challenges of life pop up, when serious illness or another crisis falls on your family, or you lose your job or experience some other financial trouble, you need someone who loves you unconditionally.

Our public lives don't always match up with our private worlds. I recently met a couple who had to combat many obstacles to live together. He, an Indian, had been Hindu though was now a Christian. She, from the Caribbean, was raised in the Pentecostal church. Everything about them, from their families, to their religion, to the food they ate, to their culture, was different. But they loved each other and each decided that the other was the person they wanted to grow old with. It is not smart to ignore differences, particularly as many as these, but they don't necessarily have to keep you from joining together. Other people may have a lot to say about who is "right" for you based on who they see you to be, but only you know for sure if someone has the qualities you need to share in your private life.

Moses had this issue thousands of years ago. "Then Miriam and Aaron spoke against Moses because of the Ethiopian woman whom he had married; for he had married an Ethiopian woman" (Numbers 12:1, NKJV). Moses' wife did not fit the profile of the person his sister Miriam thought he should marry. In fact, Miriam spoke so disrespectfully of her brother's choice that God burdened her with leprosy. This is the first instance of the disease in the Bible—not surprisingly, since Miriam was attempting to break apart what God had joined together, Moses and his beloved wife. When your union doesn't work for other people, whether it's because of race, education, religion, or social status, you have to decide, like Moses, what is right for you.

While friends and family can offer sound advice about who you should marry, be careful. Your friends and other people who know you may encourage you to choose someone who fits your lifestyle while ignoring the person who is the love of your life.

45

The Seasons of Marital Change

Like anything in life, relationships have their seasons. Sometimes you feel closer to your mate than other times. If you did your research and development in the beginning, and were clear about who you were looking for in a partner, and took a good honest look at who the person you chose is, then your union should be able to survive the warm, the cold, the sun, and the rain.

What you loved about your partner when you met doesn't usually change because you are having trouble at work or one of you is ill. But the stresses of life—even ones external to the relationship—can cause a temporary drift apart. Your relationship may just be evolving into a new season. Perhaps you need to reconnect to what caused you to fall in love in the first place, or do something to keep your union fresh and moving forward. Your mate is likely to be still the same person they were at their core, and that is the foundation of what you have together. Focusing on that essence makes the inevitable ebb and flow of life feel like the ripples of a stream rather than the crashing waves of the ocean.

Stimulation is one of the most overlooked but critical considerations in a relationship. I'm not talking about the feeling you get in the pit of your stomach when your loved one comes into the room, or the physical reaction of sexual stimulation. I mean intellectual stimulation. You sometimes need to ignite each other's imagination and renew your excitement for life and its many interesting topics.

Boredom is the cause of the death of most marriages. Partners lose their focus, stray into affairs, get addicted to porn, or exhibit other destructive behavior. I do not mean that you should excuse bad behavior, but understand that boredom is like poison that slowly seeps into every crevice of your relationship and works to kill your union.

The secret to a strong marriage is to continue to find ways to improve yourself and to share. It can be as simple as reading a book or article and sharing something interesting about what you read, or taking a course and using what you learned at home. It can be learning about your partner's career field and taking an interest in what they do all day, showing you are engaged with who they are. If you're going to marry a pro football player, then you should know something about the game. If your wife is a music industry executive, you might want to know something about the latest Billboard charts or some other music-related topic that makes you relevant to her professional world.

Partners who want to keep growing as a couple also need to have lives of their own away from the marriage as well. Pursuing hobbies, interests, and appropriate friendships outside the marriage makes each partner more interesting and stimulating when they come back home. How wonderful to sit together at the dinner table and share the exciting things you each discovered during the day. There is a balancing act in developing your own life without ignoring the life you have together.

The person you marry will be around for a very long time if you do things right. Long after physical attraction and the intensity of sexual chemistry have faded, and the kids are grown and living on their own, you and your partner will want strong connections so you can continue to grow and enjoy a life together.

46

Turn Your Marriage Around

To regain true intimacy, physical and emotional, to restore the closeness you once shared, you must be willing to allow your heart and soul to reopen. Take the risk to expose yourself to the unknown in order to reconnect as one.

To bring a marriage back from the brink of divorce is not easy; in every union there are unique considerations that must be worked out. Whether the problems in your marriage arise from external circumstances, such as losing a job or undergoing a foreclosure, or problems with the relationship, such as an affair or addiction issues, you can only rebuild by revitalizing what you once had and reconnecting with each other.

The first step in reconnecting with your mate is to practice the art of getting to know the other person. What typically happens when we are first trying to figure out someone is that we put them in a box based on who and what we think they are. Then we stick a label on the box that we hope will follow them for the rest of their lives. Truly knowing someone is not about deciding who they should be and then wanting them to stay that way forever. The mystery of knowing another requires a commitment to lifelong learning.

The Bible says that a man and a woman should dwell together according to knowledge and encourages couples to spend at least a year together without other distractions (1 Peter 3:7). Allowing time and space for you both to grow and evolve as people will be the first step toward resolving your issues.

Next is the art of listening. The reason many couples get to the place where they are considering divorce is that rather than conversations, their interactions deteriorate into sermons and monologues. Counseling can help the two of you learn to hear how the other person expresses themselves. When you are focused on being right and getting one up on the other, there is no room for solutions to emerge.

If we could learn to listen with open hearts rather than closed minds, we would have fewer divorces. Divorces happen when people's hearts get closed and hard. You must allow your heart to be vulnerable and soft in order to come to a place of understanding, where negotiation can take place. Some couples write letters to express their feelings as they navigate their way back to better and deeper communication. Just as an artist waits for the perfect light to capture a subject on canvas, couples must learn the art of waiting to help reset their relationship back on course. This requires a patience and a dedication that are not always easy but very necessary. God's timing offers us a deeper healing than anything we can construct on our own. If you are considering divorce, be sure that you have worked as hard as you can at saving your marriage, that you have exhausted every other option first.

One of the most difficult arts to master in relationships and in life is the art of forgiveness. The Lord's Prayer teaches us to "Forgive us our debts as we forgive those who are indebted to us"; other translations use "Forgive us our trespasses." Infidelity, dishonesty, and other wrongs are among the trespasses we may experience. Without the ability to practice forgiveness even for the little things, it is hard to offer or receive the grace of forgiveness. To forgive means to admit to ourselves that our partner is not perfect and neither are we.

To fail to forgive is like drinking poison and expecting the other person to die. Forgiveness not only releases your mate from your anger and hurt, it lets you out of its grasp as well. It is impossible to stay married without learning to practice forgiveness. We need it not only for each other but to have a relationship with God, since God is in us and in our union. We need forgiveness in our marriage as well.

Finally, we need to learn the art of openness and to allow ourselves to be vulnerable, transparent, and willing to trust again. The only way to deeply connect with another person is to truly allow another person to know you fully—your hopes, dreams, fears, and insecurities. It is natural, particularly after we have been hurt or rejected, to want to protect ourselves and our hearts from further pain. To do so makes perfect sense in other areas of your life, but in marriage, to close down your soul to your mate will surely lead to further pain.

Like a property growing in value over the years, your marriage builds equity over time. Like systematic investments into a savings account, small deposits add up. Your shared experience, be it the birth of your children, the day when your child drove off to begin college, the business the two of you sacrificed and saved to start, the death of your father after a long battle with cancer, or the surprise weeklong trip to the Bahamas for your birthday—it all matters. Together these things add up to a beautiful canvas of intimacy that depicts our lives.

47

Life Beyond Divorce

If you divorce, you can start over in a way that allows you to learn to love yourself and understand how to meet your own needs, sometimes for the very first time. People from all walks of life—pastors, kings and queens, princesses, CEOs, and many others—have survived divorce and gone on to have wonderful new lives. Divorce is the death of your marriage, but it doesn't have to be the death of your life. Taking time to examine your life with honesty and the new wisdom you take from the experience will help you move forward.

Staying in a relationship because you're afraid to be alone is like keeping a job that's beneath you so you don't have to engage in a challenging job search. To settle for a life as a bit player in someone else's life drama is to settle for a life of frustration and mediocrity. If you've done your due diligence on your current situation and are certain that your reasons for leaving are sound, then it's time to pursue a new dream.

Carrying the same emotional and psychological baggage from the past with you into your next relationship will only yield the same results. If you find yourself caught up in a familiar cycle of drama and dysfunction, then you need to do the work on yourself to determine why the cycle continues.

When I was a young boy, I would often jog the few blocks down to the grocery store for Mom to pick up staples like milk, bread, or eggs. What I loved most about the store was the bank of candy and machines filled with gum balls, peanuts, and toys. The machine filled with "Super Balls," which cost ten cents, was my favorite. Super Balls were little spheres, often red, blue, green, and yellow with a swirl on them. I'd bounce my newly bought treasure all the way home.

I didn't know the word at the time, but Super Balls were resilient. They were hard to break and never lost their spring. Today when someone tells me to bounce back, I think of my childhood and my Super Balls. We have to have the ability to come back for more, without losing our bounce—in fact, coming back stronger than we were before.

$-$ 48 $-$

The Job for Life—Parenting

At some point you will have to stop being the disciplinarian for your children and be their friend. But before you do, you must earn that right by being their mother or father. When children are young, they need someone to set boundaries for them and protect them from harm. Our job as parents is to act as their spiritual and moral compass.

Your children are barraged by ads, television programs, music, video games, websites, and magazines full to the brim with images of violence, sex, drug and alcohol abuse, and materialism. And much of the negative that they see is glorified and celebrated, so much so that even with a strong moral center they may begin to feel like something is wrong with them if they don't go along.

If you've ever seen the MTV program *My Super Sweet 16*, you know how bad it is. The show features sixteen-year-old boys and girls and how they live. The subjects are typically children of business executives, celebrities, or athletes. They dress in expensive designer clothing, emulating rap video stars and their scantily dressed groupies. The days of ice cream and cake and some balloons at the pizza parlor are replaced with events where the price tag sometimes tops a million dollars. Rather than a Walkman or stereo, the kids on the show get Hummers before they are even old enough to drive.

Offset these negative images by setting an example for your kids through your own behavior. You must teach them that neither life nor self-worth is defined by status symbol cars and clothes. Our children come up against many influences each day, from Facebook to iTunes, from MTV to BET; our voice is not the only one they hear. As parents, our job is to continually reinforce our beliefs and keep those other influences in the background for as long as we can, while arming our children with the tools they need to stand strong against the pressures of life.

Your childhood and your feelings about how your parents raised you will determine how you raise your children. Most of us parents at some point will vow to not make the same mistakes our parents did. But inevitably we get to the point where we hear ourselves saying or doing something they did.

You have to determine what aspects of your child-hood you want to bring with you into your adulthood, keeping those things you believed worked well, and learning from your parents' mistakes otherwise. Parenting is a lifetime commitment, there is no getting around it. As a parent you will be on call every day, all day for the rest of your life. Your social life, your family life, and your relationship with your spouse all change when you have kids.

Partnering with God to help us care for and guide our children will allow us to truly experience the joy of being a parent. The truth is, however, that you begin preparing to be a parent long before you or your partner actually gets pregnant. You must do the work to be sure you are someone ready to take a big leap of faith and open yourself to truly and unconditionally love another person. This is your job as a parent.

"Children's children are a crown to the aged, and parents are the pride of their children" (Proverbs 17:6, NIV). Deciding to become a parent is one of the most important and life-changing decisions you will ever make. Take it on with serious consideration, reverence, prayer, and a sense of humor, and parenting will be one of the greatest joys of your life.

—

Get Back
Up Again

49

Choose Your Destiny

Do you feel energized by other people? Does the support and encouragement you get from others buoy you up and make you feel strong and alive?

Or do you gain satisfaction from supporting others? Do you get a charge from reaching out to people you care about and helping them when they are in need? When your friends and loved ones show appreciation for your support, do you feel warm and fuzzy inside, satisfied that you have done something for someone else?

Both can be very gratifying. Whichever tendency you lean toward, both are a form of need. To walk in the power of your destiny, you must balance these needs by developing a strategy for the future, not one mired in history. Know that there's something you crave that is much deeper and more satisfying than either giving or receiving. It is the contentment that comes from fulfilling your God-given destiny.

You are the one who ultimately controls your own success; you are armed with the tools you need to succeed. No one else. Choosing your destiny means being clear about what stage of life you're in, your contributions and frailties, and being flexible enough to adapt to unexpected setbacks.

When you have reached a new level of success, financial solvency, or material blessing, your needs—particularly the intangible needs for love and belonging—do not go away. Who among us doesn't long to be loved and understood on a daily basis? Who among us doesn't want to be accepted or enhanced and inspired by our associations?

Put history behind you and focus on the destiny before you. You have extraordinary opportunities to feel sheltered and completed moving forward.

50

Failure Can Be Your
Biggest Blessing

It was eighty-six years before baseball's Boston Red Sox won a World Series title in 2004. Actress Susan Lucci, famously known as the fictional Erica Kane of a daytime soap opera, was nominated eighteen times before she finally won the 1999 Emmy Award for best actress in a daytime drama. Thomas Edison conducted many experiments before he developed the lightbulb. George Washington Carver spent a lifetime inventing products from his work with agricultural products like the peanut. It was nearly ten years after his first efforts before Dr. Jonas Salk developed the polio vaccine that saved countless lives.

Even though year after year they got to the dance, so to speak, but went home alone, they never stopped pursuing their dreams. Victory is often preceded by failure, sometimes numerous failures. The world is full of great people with a long list of accomplishments and a much longer list of failures. Persistence and a refusal to give up on their vision kept them coming back, and back, and back again, until they finally got what they were after.

Try to imagine what life would be like without the polio vaccine or the lightbulb. As with the small Super Balls I used to love as a child, sometimes the bounce—the rebound—is what matters most in life. Our society celebrates winners. But the truth is, just like death and taxes, failure is a part of life. It's not that successful people never get knocked down, it's just that when others are still lying on the ground nursing their wounds, winners have gotten up, dusted themselves off, and have headed back down the road toward their finish line.

Successful people pay attention to their failures and learn from them. They observe them carefully, figure out what went wrong, and use them to correct their mistakes going forward. We often begin new projects with excitement and enthusiasm. The newness of what we are doing compels us to keep moving forward. Then, inevitably, something goes wrong, and we stop. The project looked easier than it actually is, and we are not prepared to work at it and stay with it, so we quit.

My golf game, or lack thereof, is a perfect example. The truth is, I never really enjoyed playing golf. I had friends who played and they were always talking about handicaps, putting, and nine irons. What did I know? I thought tee time involved a hot beverage and some biscuits. But I started taking lessons and practiced religiously. I practiced all the time. I bought some clubs and the whole outfit, including the pants.

I liked many aspects associated with the sport—spending time in nature, on the lush, beautiful green courses, getting to interact and socialize with other men, and speeding from hole to hole in a golf cart. But those things weren't enough to keep me interested. I quickly grew tired of my lessons; in fact I started to dread going. I played less and less, until finally I allowed myself to just stop playing. I had spent a lot of time and money to learn how to play, but the truth was, I just didn't like it that much. I knew that no matter how many lessons I took and how hard I tried, I was not going to be Tiger Woods. I was Bishop Jakes, hacking at the ball like an amateur.

And that was okay with me. I could now have more informed conversations with my friends who played, because now I knew what tees and handicaps actually were. I'd gotten some good experience and had the chance to observe some of God's greatest beauty in the greens of some of the best courses in the country, but I knew for sure I didn't have what it takes to be a golfer. So many of us keep going when we know we should quit, or we decide to end a new project but feel like a loser for doing so. While the old adage says "Quitters never prosper," I actually don't think that's true. Sometimes quitters can prosper, if they make the tough decision to quit a hobby, a job, or other activity because they know it is not right for them. This is not to say that they can't learn something from their experience, like I did, but to continue with something for which they have no passion is just like throwing good money and time after bad: it's a waste.

51

Be Better, Not Bitter

Some among us seem to have more than our share of heartache and hardship. Loved ones get vicious forms of cancer or some other dreaded disease. People are forced to close their family business and file for bankruptcy, or the company they've been loyal to for twenty years downsizes and they find themselves suddenly out of work. Their childhood home catches fire and burns to the ground, or their only child is lost to street violence or war. Why do some people seem to float through life untouched by the pitfalls, while others seem to struggle with an existence that is so much more challenging and difficult?

Difficulties in life show no mercy based on who you are or who you know, and they often leave us wondering, *Why me?*

Life sometimes doesn't respond to our question, or to our desire for ease, and it rarely turns out as we'd like, but we can't just throw in the towel. We must call upon our strength to focus on those choices we can effect. We must make our lives worth living.

You may not have the money to quit your job and start your dream business, but you can sell your products part time or on the weekends. You can't resurrect your beloved grandmother after she passes, but you can keep her alive by fixing her famous sweet potato pie for Sunday dinner, and you can treat the loved ones still here on this earth with love and kindness. You may not be ready to step into that dream job, but you can go back to school to study and learn, and prepare yourself for the future. You may not have found your soul mate yet, but you can still make a meaningful life for yourself filled with supportive relationships and activities that fulfill you. You can triumph over the challenges and difficulties, even the tragedies of life. It's about attitude, sheer will, and serious determination. You simply have to choose. Am I going to call on my faith to help me keep walking toward a better future? Or am I going to give in to anger and rage and stop?

It is normal to feel anger about distressful situations. When you pretend not to feel anger and keep it locked up inside, it only manifests itself in unhealthy ways. Express your anger in a healthy way: vent to your pastor or a trusted friend, get counseling, write it in a journal. Do everything possible to expel the feelings from your system; just don't let them keep you from living the life God has planned for you.

Faith is easy when things are going well. The test is the level of faith you have when the going gets tough. You must know that God will support you and keep you and raise you up. If you have faith, God can convert the most horrific situations into fuel for tremendous and unprecedented success.

52

Retraction Comes Before Release

There was a time when Moses, called by God to speak, couldn't talk. The brilliant Albert Einstein, today considered a genius, flunked out of school. Michael Jordan was cut from his high school basketball team. Abraham Lincoln was defeated in his run for vice president and senator before becoming president of the United States.

The world's most famous overachievers first experienced some serious setbacks before they reached their glory. Instead of being knocked down by their troubles when it seemed they were down and out for the count, they turned their tragedy into triumph.

I believe this attitude explains why we often see so many immigrants from third-world countries achieve so much more than those of us who were born here in the United States. They arrive in this country hungry for an education and grateful for the opportunities we take for granted. They will juggle several jobs to make ends meet and provide for their families, while they go to school at night and study into the wee hours of the morning. Many come to this country fleeing horrific and life-threatening circumstances, yet they use that experience to spur them on.

No one attains the crown without bearing the weight of the cross. Your trainer may tell you "No pain, no gain," and it's as true at the gym as it is in your life. Sometimes you have to take two steps back before you can make a giant leap forward. This is where you assess and regroup, and ready yourself for the next leg of the journey.

Consider a cappuccino machine, like the ones you see at your favorite coffee shop. The machine is set to on to make your coffee. Steam will seep out of the valve on the side unless it is tightened. Close it up, and as the coffee brews, the pressure of the steam builds and builds. When it's ready, the barista places a plastic tube into a container of milk, unscrews the valve, and a burst of steam turns the liquid into a delicious, milky foam to top off your coffee drink. Had the steam not been restricted and kept from seeping out, it would not have been strong enough to even warm the milk.

For people who've had setbacks, sometimes having to step back and wait, regroup, and build up steam is what allows them to come out stronger than ever before. Sometimes what knocks us down eventually allows us to stand taller. Successful people know the value in staying in one place for a moment and doing the work necessary to prepare for what is coming later, even though they may have absolutely no idea what that might be.

53

Regret Can Be the Beginning of Triumph over Adversity

Few among us have always said or done the right thing one hundred percent of the time. But as we move through life and mature, hopefully we make different and better choices in our words and actions. This is the secret to not having regrets.

Maybe you were cruel or impatient with someone, and then before you could find the time to apologize, the person suddenly passed away, leaving you no chance to say you were sorry. Perhaps you lied to your spouse about something very important, and when they found out, they divorced you, feeling they could never trust you again. As a teen, you may have shoplifted something, or taken your parents' car for a joyride, and ended up spending a terrifying few hours in jail after getting caught. To this day your parents may have never forgiven you. Hopefully, you learned from your mistakes, and now, as a more conscious, self-aware person, you wouldn't do these kinds of things anymore. But you still wish you never had.

The first step to making peace with our past and the things we regret is to take responsibility for whatever it was. No matter how awful it may seem, we can rest in the assurance that there is nothing we can do to stop God from loving us. "If we confess our sins, he is faithful and just and will forgive us our sins and purify us from all unrighteousness" (1 John 1:9, NIV). If you have regrets, apologize, forgive yourself, and look to move forward in your life, smarter and more aware, and work to avoid making the same mistakes the next time.

54

Lead amid Controversy
and Conflict

One of the tasks of leadership is to accept that people
are going to see you as controversial. Exercising leadership means that many people won't understand your vision. They will criticize you and bet against you because
they can only see the world based on their own life, not
on yours. Even people in your inner circle may have trouble seeing what you see; focused on the details of their
own position, they may not be big-picture thinkers like
you are.

Leaders think in IMAX 3D, big and multidimen-
sional. What causes controversy between the leader and
the team is the chasm between a broad, global perspective and a constricted, myopic one. A strong, effective
leader can stand tall and firm in the midst of the tornado
that often accompanies misunderstanding.

As a leader you must be prepared for controversy to

come from every side of your life. Some storms you will be able to predict, and others will come at you seemingly out of nowhere. People with whom you are casually acquainted, people you see on Sunday at church, all may in fact have opinions of your work as well.

Sometimes those in your inner circle will take issue with you. If they are open and honest, these issues can usually be resolved with mature discussion. But if they agree with you in person and express disagreement to other people, that's a problem. These people defer to your title to your face but dissent behind your back. The moment you sense this kind of dynamic, respectfully but forcefully confront it.

To be a leader means you must get relatively comfortable with people being critical of your decisions. But great leaders see the big picture. They can bring warring factions together and find, somewhere in the middle, resolution.

55

Don't Settle for Mediocrity

If we can point to one important quality that distinguishes our history as a nation, it is that at some point we try to undo the wrongs we have inflicted. As a country we have faced the need to change course midway through our journey. President Lincoln knew this truth about slavery; Lyndon B. Johnson came to the same conclusion about civil rights. As one of the world's leading nations and as a democracy, we have to know when to admit our mistakes and correct course. As national issues, the residual battles of civil rights and slavery are beginning to fade as we turn toward terrorism, the war in Afghanistan, health care, immigration, and global warming as our new challenges. No matter what the fight, we must have both the intelligence to keep striving toward our future and the maturity and modesty to admit mistakes we've made in the past.

Too many of us are satisfied with mediocrity. All we ask of life is to just get by. Perhaps we have learned this attitude from past generations whose success truly was to survive the wrath of hatred and racism and make it safely home each day. But because of the sacrifice and perseverance of our ancestors, today we can ask much more of our lives. We don't want to just get by; we want excellence.

56

Take Time to Grow
into Your Harvest

We've all seen the lottery winner take home the huge jackpot, becoming an instant multimillionaire only to be poor and destitute just a few years later. Many call it the curse of the lottery. It is less a curse than a case of having too much too soon. Unlike titans of business who slowly build their financial empires over time, these lottery winners experience a sudden windfall without time to ease into their situation. As a result, they make poor choices and blow the money.

To be truly financially wealthy requires more than money; it also involves having a systematic plan in place to manage it. No matter what your goal in life, you cannot get there without learning the art of reservation in positioning yourself for success. Reservation requires patience; it involves waiting; it is about getting ready for the next opportunity to help you move closer to your goal.

It is a trait we can teach our children as well. So many kids today don't learn reservation. We see nine-year-olds with cell phone and tattoos, and twelve-year-olds having sex. It is our job as parents to protect our children and not allow them to do and have whatever they want. We need to teach them to understand that some things are appropriately reserved for adulthood, that doing certain things before you're prepared for the consequences can cause serious emotional and physical damage.

When we don't ease into our success, it can become bigger than us and eventually leave us crushed and bitter. Consider the star athlete who skips college and heads right for the pro leagues and the million-dollar contract. His family lived on food stamps and now he is driving a Bentley and wearing shoes that cost more than his mother earns in a year as a maid. It's never surprising to read the headlines in the newspaper about him getting involved in drugs or mixed up with violence or some other crime. Or think of the VH1 television program *Behind the Music.* The names are different, but the story is almost always the same: young kid from the streets or the trailer park gets discovered, gets a record deal, skyrockets to fame, gets involved with drugs and alcohol and the wrong people, and the artist's star crashes as fast as it rose.

Waiting for your success, preparing for it, doesn't

mean that you miss a benefit, it just means you're wise. Develop good financial habits to manage the bigger salary you will get with the big promotion. Get your home in order. Make it inviting, so that you're ready to host a romantic dinner when you find the special someone you seek. Make sure you understand what sacrifices and changes you will have to make to accommodate the goals you've set.

In the reserved season, God is allowing you time to prepare for the riches he plans to shower on your life. True wealth rarely manifests without a long road of hard work. In order for the wealth to endure, we must cherish and honor it.

—

Live Your
Dream

57

You Are the Leader of Your Life

Leaders draw attention to themselves in the things they say and do because they tend to think and act differently from most people. Their decisions tend to create conflict. But they know that to be decisive often means not winning a popularity contest.

Commitment is a leader's middle name. Vision is a leader's stock in trade. Leaders go after what they want with laser focus on the finish line. And they don't allow drama and the obstacles that pop up along the way to deter them.

In everything they do, their character is their guide. Leaders know who they are and what they stand for, and their actions are born from those traits. Honesty, integrity, tenacity, and flexibility are all character traits of good leaders.

You are the leader of your own life. And it is up to

you to guide your life as if you were running a company that you want to be wildly successful. In order to do so, you will need to worry less about popularity than you do about policy—your personal life plan for success. A mother teaches her children the power of helping others when they volunteer as a family at the soup kitchen on Saturdays—whether the children are happy about the idea or not. A couple teach their children about resolving conflict by calmly discussing their differences of opinion rather than screaming, yelling, and name-calling when they argue. A night supervisor refuses to gossip about coworkers; a coffee shop barista serves every cup of joe with a smile and a "have a nice day," no matter how surly his customer may be.

Jesus showed his leadership by example in the way he treated others. You don't have to be a CEO, a minister, or a president to be a leader. We can all make the choice to be a leader in our life, through how we treat the people in our life. Whether it be your coworkers, fellow churchgoers, the person behind the counter at the grocery checkout, the guy who picks up the recycling each week, family, friends, and even people you consider your enemies—as a leader, you treat everyone in your life with the respect with which you would want to be treated.

58

Dream Fulfillment Requires
a Firm Commitment

We all have that little voice inside, the authentic voice that tells us the truth about our life. The voice calls out to us, even when we stop listening and have stopped answering when she calls. Occasionally we hear something and wonder, *What was that noise?* Sometimes we pause in the midst of work and family obligations and the rest of our busy lives, but then we march ahead, convincing ourselves we haven't heard anything. The spirit behind the voice is desperate to get our attention. It is aware that we don't realize that each day we drift further and further away from her, settling for less than what we know to be our true desires and capabilities, letting go of the creative pursuits that once brought us joy and were the key to a future of meaning and fulfillment, all in exchange for a "responsible" life and roles that others have assigned to us. The voice is the sound of the dreams you had for yourself. She is the one who knows the big plans you had for your life, your ambitions to be a great success.

She remembers when you imagined being so much more, when you wanted to expand beyond your circumstances and live a life of richness and meaning, filled with great love and joy.

The voice loves you unconditionally. She hates to see you struggle with sadness and regret, living a life of quiet desperation as you sleepwalk your way through your many work and family obligations, and taking in very little, if any, joy from your existence. *"Who are you?"* she screams. *"What do you want? Why have you stopped listening to me, to your inner voice, to God?"*

Of course, you did not intentionally turn away from her; it happened gradually over the years. For a long time you desperately listened for her, clinging to any small sound from within that told you life could be what you once believed. As life transpired, and you found yourself surrounded by people who didn't know you, who didn't see the dreams inside, and who put you down, she tried to come to your aid, yelling to support you and remind you that you could be whatever you wanted. But you got tired of struggling and told her she didn't understand. You turned your back on her.

Finally she got tired of trying to get your attention.

For a long time she was quiet. And then she got angry. After all, she was always there for you, she never left you, but all she ever heard you say was that you were all alone, that no one cared about you or supported you. The truth is, she was always there, and the lies you told about her hurt her. She was hurt that she tried so hard to help you but you wouldn't let her. All the voice could do was watch you become more and more negative and angry. It made her cry to see your cynicism about life, when she knew that you once saw the world as bursting with possibilities.

She takes in a deep breath, braces herself, and then screams as loud as she can, "You don't have to live this way! Listen to me, the voice inside you. Turn away from the world and look within. I am still here, your God-given voice, and I can help you!" Your happiness is with her—your voice, your dreams, and your God.

Learning Is a Process, Not a Product

Life can get hectic. Sometimes, rather than being in charge of our life, we find life in charge of us. When that happens, the best thing we can do for ourselves is just stop. To recharge and regroup is often all we need to find the lost enthusiasm for life. When we know we need it but can't find time to do it, we feel frustrated.

Journeys take time; they are sometimes slow and painful. But as with losing weight or saving for the down payment for a dream home, there are hurdles we must clear along the way in order to reach our final destination. Once there, we can look back and appreciate all we went through. One of the keys to getting where we want to go is faith. When you are headed down the road and suddenly a huge mountain stands between you and where you are trying to go, it takes belief in yourself to make the climb. Faith is required because you can't see what's on the other side and know for sure that you will be happy about what's really there.

Living is a process in which learning and growth are an integral part. The way to achieve is to step out on faith. While we may want to know what is going to happen, believing that we can prepare, the truth is life is always full of surprises. The journey teaches us resilience, patience, understanding, and perseverance. A lot is required and we may need a respite along the way, and that's okay. Sometimes we get bleary-eyed after driving too long and we need to pull off to the side of the road and take a nap. We wake feeling refreshed, alert, and ready to head back down the road.

Your partner may or may not share your vision. Only you can decide whether or not you want and need to be with someone who does. Not everyone will have the faith and belief in where you are going, and sometimes a partner's lack of faith makes the trip all the more challenging. Sometimes our partners only go along because they love us, but they too have lives and can sometimes get burned out by trying to support us.

Be aware of those around you and show gratitude for what they do to support you. Smart couples become students of their own success. With every little victory they consider what they learned from it, how they grew. And they take that learning and use it as they move forward. I am not talking about going back to school to earn a degree or taking an online course, although formal education is always a good idea. I mean the lessons you learn in the school of hard knocks, where life is the school and the lessons are what we learn along the way.

60

Cultivate a Well-Rounded Life

We must invest in relationships with the same gusto as we do our business lives. To thrive in life you must come up with a long-term plan based on your needs, those of your loved ones, and your long-term vision for your life.

Offering financial support to our loved ones is necessary and important, but thriving relationships also require an investment of our personal time and physical presence. Further, you can physically be with others but be disconnected, checking emails or sending text messages back to the office. It takes effort to strike that important balance between work and home life, but the balance is essential to the health of either relationship. No amount of money can replace a face-to-face conversation, a hug, or simply just showing up for a loved one.

Success often requires long hours and sacrifice. Something always suffers as a result, and it is often those all-important personal relationships. Statistics show workweeks of fifty hours plus are the norm for nearly one quarter of U.S. workers, while almost that same number say they work six or seven days a week.

So how do we do it? How do we meet our business goals and maintain a healthy family life? Many companies today implement work-life balance programs in an effort to help employees find that middle ground. They offer work-at-home scenarios, flexible schedules, onsite day care, and other benefits to help employees maintain personal lives. It's a smart move. You've heard the phrase "Happy wife, happy life." It also applies to happy children, happy boyfriends, and so on. Make your home life as much of a priority as your business life.

61

Keep the Main Thing
the Main Thing

In the 1980 winter Olympics the underdog American hockey team, a scrappy group of college players, took on the mighty Soviet Union in the semifinals. The Russians, favored to win the gold medal, were a powerhouse group of players who had been playing together for many years. They dominated the international hockey world with their strength and skill. Out of nowhere, on their home turf in Lake Placid, New York, the Americans beat the Russians and, in a game dubbed the Miracle on Ice, went on to win the gold medal against Finland. The crowd and the nation went wild over this unknown group of young men. It was a story of overcoming the odds, teamwork, and pure determination—an American story.

When he stepped up to the podium to accept the gold medal on his team's behalf, team captain Mike Eruzione frantically waved for them all to join him on the tiny pedestal. It was a heartwarming sight to see the entire team clamor excitedly out onto the ice to join him on the top step while the national anthem played. Eruzione knew this medal belonged to all of them, and he wanted to be sure the world knew it too.

Particularly when you are the leader, whether it be the leader of your family or of your team at work or of a group in church, it is your job to create a space where people feel welcomed and loved.

Today's powerful women want especially to focus on this principle. So many sisters today are soaring to heights our ancestors never could have imagined. You are doctors and lawyers and corporate CEOs. The men in your life may feel like you are leaving them behind. It is not always easy for a man to mix and mingle with his wife's investment bank colleagues when he spends his days unloading trucks at the grocery store. Unloading trucks is a good, honest living, and there's not a thing wrong with that job, but sometimes others make it known by the looks on their faces or their body language that they don't think he belongs.

My advice is to put out that flame before it gets a chance to burn. Spend some time telling your coworkers who your husband is as a man. How you wouldn't be close to where you are now if it weren't for his unwavering love and support. Put a stop to the sideways glances or rolling of the eyes by inviting your husband up to the gold medal step with you.

Success means very little if you don't have people close to you to share it with. You want to be careful that as you climb up the ladder, you don't leave your loved ones behind. Talking at home about your work is another way to avoid difficult situations later. Plus it helps your family understand what you do and feel a part of it. They can also offer support at home, knowing when you have a huge presentation or some other stressful situation at the office. They don't have to understand every detail of what you do, but share enough with them that they can feel at home in your work world.

You couldn't have made it to where you are without the support of your loved ones. Don't make them irrelevant once you reach your goal. It is great to be a success, but you never hear anyone on their deathbed say that they regret that they didn't work more or earn more money. Keep your desire for success in perspective and in balance with the things in your life that really matter—God, family, home, and health. These are the things that make for a real life, the main thing that we are working for in the first place. It seems obvious, but we often ignore the very people we are striving so hard to succeed for. Build your home and your life on the foundation of infinite love.

Also remember, it's not all about you! The people in your life are not just extras in your career drama. They have lives of their own. Focusing on the needs of others, whether it be your spouse, your children, or extended family members and friends, keeps you from being so self-involved. Show up for them, as you need them to support you. Whether it's for the school play or a weekend soccer game, a wedding, a bar mitzvah, or a milestone anniversary, making the time to celebrate the achievements in the lives of others makes you a well-rounded person. It keeps you from forgetting that you are not in this alone. When they sense that you don't support them as much as they give to you, people feel taken advantage of. Showing interest in others will make it more likely that they will want to support you when you need it, and everyone needs that, whether they have the corner office or not.

Prepare for a Smooth Landing

As you know if you've ever flown on a plane, it is the landing that's most likely to be a bit bumpy. Even the most frequent flier takes note of the sudden drops in altitude a pilot often has to make to avoid certain wind and weather conditions when bringing the plane in for a landing. Careers can cause the same kind of commotion in our home life. While you may be concerned with board meetings and strategic plans, the members of your family often have their own concerns—homework, school dances, and trips to visit their sister's new baby. And those are as important to them as your meeting with the regional vice president is to you.

Consider a professional athlete at the end of his career. Used to the glare and the constant attention of the spotlight, he now spends his time at home helping wash the dishes and taking out the trash. That's quite a leap from the limelight. The bird that once soared can't find a place to land, and it crashes to the ground, tired of flapping its wings.

Smooth landings in life require some planning and forethought. Just as a pilot can't just suddenly decide to drop a plane straight from the sky down to the ground, when you are making a significant shift in life, where possible, take it slow. In order for the descent to be smooth, you must take your time. If you plan to retire, for example, will you stay in the home you own, or downsize to a smaller place? These are questions you have to start to ask yourself long before the day of the retirement party.

I've heard countless wives complain that their husbands are driving them crazy being around the house so much after they retire. Wives too have their routines at home during the day, and they may feel a bit invaded by a husband who now has much more time on his hands. If you're newly retired, you will have to find a way to slowly integrate yourself back into the household routine and find a new role for yourself.

Adjusting to new circumstances takes a while. You have to learn how to ease your plane into the hangar. You may have desired a time when you didn't have a day-to-day heavily packed schedule but find that it takes you longer than expected to slow your pace, much less do nothing. You don't want to end up like the people who land back in jail because the outside world is too overwhelming. They like the idea of being free, but they miss the routine and safety of a jail cell and hot meals.

63

Check Your Reality

Sometimes we lose touch with our roots or become too caught up in our new life to stay connected to our old one. Visiting family for holidays and other special occasions is no longer a priority.

Some of us start to think we have nothing in common with those we left behind; we get caught up in our self-importance. We forget how the people back home supported us, cheered for us, and helped us become who we are today. Once defined by our parents, friends, and neighbors, we are now defined by the corporate culture, international flights, designer handbags, seventy-hour workweeks, who we know, and where we are going.

When this is the world you live in, it can be hard to transition back into the life you left behind. Returning to a place you felt was too small for you can be trying. It's hard to look back at our past lives, particularly when the memories may be painful. It is not uncommon to feel like you have grown and changed so much but those you left behind are still in the same spot.

There are also those back home who can't wait to tell you that you are not who you were. Your mere presence makes them feel inferior or superior. They treat you like a stranger, like they don't know you anymore. And that can hurt. We know how important our friends and family are even when our life has changed. Once you've tasted the sweetness of success, you often find yourself feeling more alone. You don't fit in with the country club crowd, but you don't fit in at Joe's Chicken Shack anymore either. Sometimes success can be lonely, and connecting with people who understand that can be difficult.

Often the solution lies in your behavior. Reaching out to your family and friends and relating to them about things they care about is a good beginning. While they may not appreciate the beauty of fine linens and gourmet food, your boys back home still love to watch the game on Sunday and reminisce about the local championship when you were all on the team. Connecting to people where they are—physically or mentally—is the key to maintaining solid relationships. Keep your roots tended to, and they will be the support you need to continue to grow into the mighty oak you were meant to be.

64

Celebrate!

Celebrate and allow yourself to be celebrated. Regularly make the effort to create surprises and initiate thoughtful gestures—an unexpected card in the mail, flowers at the office, or a pair of coveted tickets to the theater or a sports event. Never stop making those around you feel special. Maintain the excitement of relationships, and combat boredom.

We all need encouragement and special attention. Life can sometimes be challenging and get us down. The celebration I am talking about is not necessarily a party, although throwing a party or other gathering in honor of someone you care about is a thoughtful thing to do. Fundamentally, the point is to give attention to what is important to other people in your life.

When they were growing up, did their family make a big deal out of birthdays? Do they send cards and flowers to other people on their birthdays? Do they love nature or enjoy walking after a beautiful snowfall or smelling the sweet scent of roses? Is your mate a type A person who can't sit still and likes to be active and on the go? Or does your partner enjoy relaxing with a good book and a steaming hot cup of tea? Are they positive or negative? Do they see the glass in life as half empty or half full?

To celebrate someone includes offering comfort when they need it. One of the greatest skills in life is not only to be able to enjoy the good times, but also to be able to find something to celebrate about each other every day, even when life is not so great.

Recall how you felt as a child on the morning of your birthday. The night before you could barely sleep while you anticipated the party you would have, all of your friends from school who would be there, your aunts, uncles, cousins, and of course your beloved grandparents, who always made you feel like the most special person on the face of the earth.

While we are older and more mature now, we all still have that little kid inside, and we want to be celebrated and we need to be. It's nice to be the object of the attention. Whether it is for big celebrations like birthdays, anniversaries, and job promotions, or celebrating the smaller things in life that only matter to you, making your loved ones feel special and cherished in ways that matter to them creates long-lasting bonds that help you live a life without limits.